Praise for
A Learner's Paradise

"This book offers a fresh and engaging overview of the New Zealand education system with provocations and practical suggestions for the classroom teacher, whether international or local. There is a clear emphasis on New Zealand's learner-centric approach which positions both teachers and students as lifelong learners who inquire, explore, and grow in a high-trust model. New Zealanders will be reminded of just how lucky they are, and international educators will be inspired to adapt best-practice examples for their own context. Written with Richard's typical gentle sense of humour, this is a highly enjoyable and thought-provoking read."

—**Philippa Nicoll Antipas**, Connected Learning Advisor,
CORE Education, @AKeenReader

"Richard Wells paints a powerful portrait of what learning looks like in New Zealand and encourages educators to reflect and act on how they can move forward within their own schools. These narratives from around the world help create a story of what is possible in schools today no matter where you are in the world."

—**George Couros**, division principal of Innovative Teaching and Learning,
Parkland School Division, @gcouros

"In a desperate search for innovation in twenty-first-century education, Richard Wells decided to take a look at the New Zealand public school system. His book, A Learner's Paradise, explores the initiatives that his country has put into place which challenge the status quo and foster a forward-thinking approach to putting students on a successful path to lifelong learning. I hope everyone interested in the futures of all young people will take the opportunity to read this book."

—**C. M. Rubin**, author, *The Global Search for Education*

A Guidebook for Parents and Educators Everywhere

A
Learner's
Paradise

How New Zealand Is
Reimagining Education

Richard Wells

I must dedicate this book to my
wife and daughters for putting
up with my obsessions with
education and allowing me to
spend hours at my laptop.
I love you all!

A Learner's Paradise
©2016 by Richard Wells

This book is available at special discounts when purchased in quantity for use as premiums, promotions, fundraising, and educational use. For inquiries and details, contact us: edtechteam.com/press.

Published by EdTechTeam Press

Cover Design by Genesis Kohler
Editing and Interior Design by My Writers' Connection

Library of Congress Number: 2016944954
Paperback ISBN: 978-1-945167-10-2
E-book ISBN: 978-1-945167-11-9

First Printing: June 2016

Contents

Chapter 1

How I Accidently Discovered the Best Education System in the World

Originally from England, I started my teaching career in the United Kingdom in 2003. After my training, which primarily focused on surviving in a hostile classroom and marking, I was delighted to discover that the UK government had recently introduced an information communication technology (ICT) curriculum. As a newly qualified teacher specialising in ICT, I felt fortunate at the time to be handed, due to excellent funding, a full set of resources with lesson plans and accompanying CDs of PowerPoint presentations to deliver to the students. *Wow!* I thought, *this is easy!*

Seven minutes into "Lesson One," I sensed a reduction in enthusiasm for "Traffic light control systems." And so began my *real* teaching career.

I'll cover my move to New Zealand in more detail later, but it started with a relatively easy shift to a private school in Auckland. I say *easy* because the school was using the UK-styled Cambridge International Examinations, not the Kiwi (Kiwi is the colloquial term for New Zealand) system, so it required no change for me in approach or content. It was at this school in 2009, where I had my second restart to my teaching career, when a high school student raised his hand and politely asked:

"Could you please, please, please *stop talking*?"

He delivered the request so softly and sincerely, and notice—that's three pleases! This five-second moment sent me into a twenty-four-hour tailspin of questioning my purpose as a teacher and why education had me acting as a sort of awkward information-delivery machine. Was there another option?

I had to get through the extensive list of content on the Cambridge curriculum. I had to prepare the students for their three-hour examinations. Surely, there was no other option than to stand at the front of the room and continue talking, delivering, and clicking through PowerPoint slides.

In a desperate search for a solution that wouldn't put my students to sleep, I decided to take a good look at the New Zealand system from which I was shielded by the beautiful red brick walls of this private school. The new national curriculum had been placed in every teacher's pigeonhole, and so I grabbed my copy and was surprised to see the ICT reduced to a single paragraph. My first thought was, *Well, that's shortsighted.* But then I noticed that the math curriculum didn't even fill a page. *Hang on; this is weird,* I thought. *How does this educate a country? Where does a teacher start? Surely, the teachers don't decide what to teach!*

Thus, I embarked on an exploration of a whole new approach to running an education system. Trusting the teachers to fill and maintain the curriculum framework with appropriate content was just one of many major differences I learned to appreciate.

In 2011, I began connecting with educators around the world online through my blog and on Twitter. Now, in 2016, I can see in global conversations that teachers around the world have the same difficulties I did in my early years of teaching with prescribed curriculum content lists and standardised exam preparation. Those conversations, and the frustration behind them, are what compelled me to introduce the world to just how different and rewarding education can be when teachers are trusted to do their jobs. During the past seven years, I've seen this approach lead to amazing initiatives and excellent experiences for both learners and educators.

I believe that every country needs a more flexible and personalised education system because the old, more simple, twentieth-century divisions and hierarchies have all but disappeared. As Eddie Obeng explains in his TED Talk,[1] it's as if the rules that govern how everything in the world operates were scrapped in the year 2000, "whilst we were all sleeping." It is this idea of change—which educational systems worldwide have missed or ignored—that compelled me to write this book.

Here are four examples of things that, in 1999, were not expected to happen in just three years:

1. A college graduate[2] becomes CEO of a multinational company at the age of twenty-four.

2. A seven-year-old[3] starts to earn more than five million dollars a year by making online videos.

---

1   "Eddie Obeng: Smart failure for a fast-changing world |
    TED ..." 2014. 20 Feb. 2016, https://www.ted.com/talks/
    eddie_obeng_smart_failure_for_a_fast_changing_world
2   "Mark Zuckerberg - Wikipedia, the free encyclopedia." 2011. 25 Apr. 2016,
    https://en.wikipedia.org/wiki/Mark_Zuckerberg
3   "EvanTubeHD - YouTube." 2011. 25 Apr. 2016,
    https://www.youtube.com/user/EvanTubeHD

3. An entire global industry that existed for more than 100 years collapses due to a service[4] unachievable three years previous.
4. The average employee considers not just a new job but also a new career.[5]

The four examples above are events and social issues that most, if not all, formal education systems do not tackle directly. Thousands of teachers are doing a great job discussing and working on these types of challenges. Unfortunately, this discussion often occurs in spite of the system, not because of it, which means that a young person's experience and understanding of trends and challenges in twenty-first-century life is ad hoc and not guaranteed. If we are to truly prepare young people for a future world we know little about, it will require a turnaround on many of the mindsets and values that govern people's approach to education.

I have discussed New Zealand's education system with people from many different countries both online and in person. I have presented the topic in the United States and held webcam conferences about it. These varied audiences almost always show amazement at what we are doing, and invariably a few people tell me they'd love to move here immediately. It was during one of these Google Hangouts that a participant suggested I write a book to outline New Zealand's education system in more detail.

Rather than flood the book with my opinions, I have attempted to outline as objectively as I can how education operates in New Zealand. You will read about some of the amazing achievements as well as the various struggles that you might expect to occur in the transition from fixed, well-ingrained, and conventional educational culture to a

---

4 "Uber | Sign Up to Drive or Tap and Ride." 2011. 25 Apr. 2016, https://www.uber.com/
5 "Job Hopping Is the 'New Normal' for Millennials - Forbes." 2012. 25 Apr. 2016, http://www.forbes.com/sites/jeannemeister/2012/08/14/job-hopping-is-the-new-normal-for-millennials-three-ways-to-prevent-a-human-resource-nightmare/

practice that is future ready, student centred, and flexible all the way from kindergarten to high school graduation. I have also indicated the extent or progress we have made on each issue. In some aspects, we are well down the line into futuristic stuff; in other areas we have only laid the foundation. However, it's important to note that, when we look at all the systems as a whole, New Zealand might have education sewn up better than any other country in the world.

Through the course of many conversations with frustrated yet hopeful educators, I've come to believe that the world needs to see how New Zealand's education system and its initiatives are solving so many fundamental problems. My intent isn't to brag or boast, but to share best practices with others so that learners and teachers around the world will benefit from the Kiwi experience. That is why I found myself in a café in Auckland, tapping away on my laptop whilst working on this book. I hope you enjoy it.

Why Read This Book?

We all know education could be better. As teachers, most of us have thought about the need for improvement in education, dwelling on the problem for a moment before putting it to one side. Education is such a big animal—the thought of grappling with it can seem overwhelming.

Regardless of where you teach, I'm sure you are aware of obvious problems. You may be certain that those problems are solvable—but not under the current administration or with the public's prevailing mindset towards education. In fact, teachers often resign themselves to the idea that, give or take a few elements, all countries experience the same kinds of issues, and it's just the way it is. Only that isn't true, and that's why I have written this book.

I want to let you in on a secret: Someone's worked it all out! Now, when I say "worked it all out," I mean that all the required components for an excellent, forward-thinking, effective educational system are already in place. The only obstacles to overcome in order to benefit from this flexible approach are mindset and understanding. Let's be clear to start with: This book is about New Zealand, but I promise not to mention anything about Hobbits, rugby, or small flightless birds. These are the things that people commonly associate with New Zealand. The goal of this book is to add another item to the list: education. In this book, I aim to paint a true picture of what it's like to work in a country where the education system has all the essential building blocks in place to lead the world of formal learning for many years to come. I will share the secrets of how New Zealand has managed to develop and continue to grow a forward-thinking, future-ready, public education system.

This book is for you if you...

- Are wondering how even high schools could operate without classrooms or lessons!
- Need reassurance that new pedagogies can work on a national scale
- Are tired of testing students to within an inch of their lives and are wondering how your country could ever move away from standardised tests
- Need to convince the public, your administrators, and maybe your friends that trusting teachers and students to run education can work for a country
- Need an example of an education system operating with an intrinsic motivation to improve itself without those external carrots or sticks
- Teach in New Zealand and aren't aware of how lucky you are, or you just want to know more about what's going on
- Wish you could move to New Zealand because you're fed up with your country, state, district, or school's ineffective system
- Want examples of how sorting out one fundamental element of an education system can have a positive ripple effect on the other elements that currently cause frustration for thousands of teachers worldwide

Around the world, educators and administrators are questioning the direction in which education should be heading. Some governments, I feel, are unfortunately pushing it in the wrong direction. My dream is that this book will act as a blueprint for other countries to start redesigning their education systems. I hope, too, that wherever you are in education—the classroom, administration, or government— that you'll use the ideas and information in this book to improve students' learning experiences. Today's young people live in a world that operates with so many unpredictable influences on fundamentals like employment, economy, migration, and the environment. They need the best education we can give them.

For Whom Is This Book Written?

If you have anything to do with education, there will be something in here for you. Perhaps you are a board member, principal, or teacher and are looking for a tangible example of how public education can be better. As you seek to bring about change in your area, please note that, in this book, I am referring to public education. In some countries, private schools have the edge on education. In contrast, the strong structure that is in place in New Zealand has left our private schools struggling to keep up. Their struggle is less with resourcing; private schools in New Zealand have very nice swimming pools, running tracks, and old-style brick buildings. My discussions and experience show me that private schools grapple with change due to the effect it has on branding and the threat it might have on their client base. Before you assume that ample resources are necessary to create a learner's paradise, I want to set the record straight. This book is about how the public schools of an entire nation are developing their pedagogy and future-readiness *without* the need for huge cash injections.

I want to inform people about how New Zealand schools are greatly focused on what students are doing and being challenged with. My excitement is about collaborative educators making decisions in partnership with administrators and about students negotiating their own paths through education. If you are interested in how these things are blossoming and how the seeds were sown in the first place, then carry on reading.

This book is also aimed at New Zealanders. If you are a Kiwi, I hope this book reminds you of just how lucky you are to live and work here. You may be surprised to learn just how difficult it is for teachers in other parts of the world and how they would dream of some of the freedoms we take for granted. As a leader in a high school—who now interviews and employs young new teachers who, unlike me, have been trained to teach the Kiwi way—it's fun for me to witness how excited and also challenged they are by having to collaborate with colleagues to design their students' school experience entirely, even through to the final high school assessments. I hope this book is useful for new Kiwi teachers too, in outlining many of these great initiatives available to us as well as the best practice going on around the country.

Because my personal experience is high school based, much of the information and many of the examples in this book come from that perspective. What I hope will interest teachers of other age groups is that I'll also explain how making high school education and assessment flexible and personalised allows the middle and elementary schools to do the same. With that kind of secondary level experience in place, teachers at the middle school and elementary levels are freed from the sense that they are preparing students for a standardised and test-driven future. This freedom has an impact on all education, including kindergarten.

Disclaimer and Vocabulary

I've tried to give a frank account about what it's like to be a New Zealand educator and an honest look at how the development of a futuristic education system can be messy and clouded in confusion, however wonderfully successful it might be currently. The views are personal and not that of my employer, government, and certainly not all New Zealand educators.

To save constant translation, I will stick with American terms when referring in general to educational stages such as elementary, middle school, high school, etc. In New Zealand, a *college* is a university, a high school is a college, a middle school is an intermediate (sort of), and an elementary is a primary. However, and here is where it gets tricky, in the event of referring to an actual institution, I will have to use its name. So Kia Aroha College is a high school, and Taupaki Primary is an elementary, and so on. Do your best to remember I'm using American terms except when referring to actual school names, or it will get very confusing. Good luck!

Why I Flew to a Flightless Land

Until people arrived in New Zealand about 700 years ago,[6] the islands had no mammals. Many of the birds that lived here lost their ability to fly due to a lack of predators. Be it penguins on the coast or Kakapo parrots on land, our indigenous birds don't act like those in other places. These ground-dwelling birds were an easy meal for both humans and the mammals they brought with them, and thus became increasingly rare. Its rarity and flightless attributes are what make our Kiwi bird famous and why New Zealanders are referred to as "Kiwis."

I have not always been a Kiwi. I arrived with my family in 2006 from the United Kingdom. You may be questioning such a big move to the other side of the globe as much as I did during transit, but here's the quick version of events. My wife, Kathryn, and I are both English and taught in UK high schools. When we had our first child in 2005, Kathryn's brother was busy doing his overseas experience or "OE," as Kiwis call it, in some tiny, far-off land, where, judging by the pictures, you had to climb mountains, ski, or whitewater raft to get anywhere. Since he wasn't at home to meet his first niece, we flew to New Zealand for three weeks. It was July and, according to the tourist brochures, we were to experience the New Zealand winter. Expecting English-style

---

6 "When was New Zealand first settled? – Te Ara Encyclopedia ..." 2009. 20 Feb. 2016, http://www.teara.govt.nz/en/when-was-new-zealand-first-settled

grey weather, we were amazed to enjoy twenty-one days of sun whilst exploring both of its beautiful islands.

The people were friendly, relaxed, and particularly active. They seemed to have more time and reason to enjoy life to its full, making the most of the vast range of climates and environments available in this small country. Even walking past school playgrounds in Auckland, we noticed this more adventurous approach to life with children climbing trees (an activity that is banned on UK school grounds) and open-gate policies because there was no need for strict security measures regarding who could and couldn't be on school grounds.

As educators in the United Kingdom, not too far from Cambridge, we knew a different kind of school. We knew coded gates, strict rules enforcing restrictions around play, and a lifestyle that was not encouraging many children to explore and discover—especially outdoors. By the end of the three weeks, Kathryn and I had decided that it seemed to make more sense to bring up our children in New Zealand. At the very least, it was certainly worth a go.

A job appeared online at a top private high school in Auckland. I interviewed over webcam and was offered the position. We were lucky that, in 2006, New Zealand needed teachers. The private school at which I worked for six years provided a gentle introduction into New Zealand education, as it used both the UK's A-level system and the local qualification, New Zealand Certificate in Educational Achievement (NCEA). This gave me six years to carry out a direct comparison of the two very different approaches.

After four years at a private school, I started to realise how much opportunity was being lost running a foreign, more traditional alternative. I moved to a public school after my sixth year in New Zealand, and since then have come to appreciate the flexibility and future-readiness of this country's curriculum and assessment system. What follows is my explanation of the current New Zealand education system, the challenges it still faces, and why I believe it is the best in the world.

Questions for Readers

1. Are you proud of your country's education system?

2. Is your system driven by assessment that honours the whole individual?

3. Sir Ken Robinson's 2006 TED Talk[7] is one of the most viewed education resources in recent times. How has your country shown appreciation for the topics it raises?

---

7 Do Schools Kill Creativity?, TED Talk, Feb. 2006,
   https://www.ted.com/talks/ken_robinson_says_schools_kill_creativity

Chapter 2
New Zealand Finds a New Approach

Growing new education is a messy business. I don't want to bore you with too much history and politics, but I think it's important to give you a brief background into how New Zealand got to where it is today. In the 1980s, New Zealand had a big problem: Between the late 1960s and late 1980s, 40 percent of New Zealanders left school with no qualification.[1] As concern grew, the government produced reports that promoted the idea that competition between self-governing schools would be an excellent way to raise the quality of education. The country launched the "Tomorrow's Schools" policy, which focused on administration more than learning. It brought about both bad and good results. On the bad side, the policy hastily shifted budgetary, employment, and property administration to each school without much preparation or direction, leaving them to "invent it as

---

1 "Who achieves what in secondary schooling? A ... - PPTA." 2014. 20 Feb. 2016, http://ppta.org.nz/membershipforms/doc_view/1648-who-achieves-what-in-secondary-schooling-a-conceptual-and-empirical-analysis

they went along."[2] At the time, this self-governance also showed "no evidence that giving schools control of their budgets and employment decisions per se has led to system-wide gains in student performance or learning."[3] The policy did bring competition that, unfortunately, soured relationships between schools. Although much of this competitive culture has died away, it still occasionally pops up in the news, even now.[4]

A Silver Lining to Self-Governance

On the good side, this neoliberal-style policy introduced a new approach to the governance of individual schools: full autonomy, with schools being governed solely by their own boards. This policy change was the first significant step towards the government and the public trusting educators to run education and make decisions to use the curriculum that best suited their particular students.

High school curriculum choices continued to be limited, conforming to the needs of externally marked national exams for sixteen to eighteen year olds until reform around high school graduation came in 2004. That being the case, there were improvements at the high school level. For example, many high schools have a student representative on the board, a point of school governance that may seem alien to many countries. The student's presence keeps the learner's perspective visible in debates on any decision.

The changes that came as a result of the Tomorrow's Schools policy sound great but, as many educators around the world can attest, allowing schools to make operational decisions has little impact on

2   "Tomorrow's Schools 'lost a decade' | Stuff.co.nz." 2012. 21 Feb. 2016, http://www.stuff.co.nz/national/education/8030433/ Tomorrows-Schools-lost-a-decade

3   WYLIE, C. "a 'self-managed schools' - Victoria University of Wellington." 2012, http://www.victoria.ac.nz/education/research/nzaroe/issues-index/2009/ pdf/text-Wylie.pdf

4   "Parents take extreme measures to move children out of ..." 2015. 20 Feb. 2016, http://www.stuff.co.nz/national/education/73732596/ Parents-take-extreme-measures-to-move-children-out-of-school-zones

education if the curriculum and assessment are still standardised and decisive over the education taking place.

By the time we reached the twenty-first century, the concept of educators operating their own schools was quite ingrained in New Zealand. Driven by a need to cater to more types of learners, and in doing so improve school leavers' qualification status, the focus turned to learning and assessment. Discussions about modernising the overall curriculum began at the government level, with the initiative being to tackle the unsatisfactory levels of unqualified school leavers by reviewing and introducing a new approach to high school qualifications.

Starting the national curriculum review with a completely new approach to senior high school assessment is important if you want to modernise whole-system change. The learning environment teachers create is strongly influenced by what they know the students will have to tackle in future school settings. The exams and assessments with which graduating students are confronted have a trickle-down effect on lower grades. In 2015, I ran a project with middle school teachers in which our discussions covered the restrictions on personalising the middle school learning experience brought about by a perceived need to prepare them for more standardised high school assessment. Likewise, elementary teachers can feel very pressured in preparing their more senior students for the experience of testing in middle schools.

By deciding to tackle the issue with final exams, New Zealand completely reformed the country's new education structure. In an attempt to reduce the number of students leaving school without qualifications, the government established a more flexible system. This new approach allowed teachers to tailor courses for their students and make decisions about how they would obtain credit for each element or topic they were assessing, so as to construct an overall qualification. In 2002, tenth-grade students were to use the standard-based assessment, whilst students in the two grades above them would be phasing out the old system. The new system was titled National Certificate in

Educational Achievement (NCEA). Teams of teachers across the country produced a library of competency and knowledge standards, which were moderated by other educators. Schools, their departments, and even individual teachers were free to develop courses from this library. The academic demand of this first-level qualification was purposefully set lower to catch more of the failing students and give them opportunity to leave school with some sort of record of achievement. (I will go through the specifics and examples of NCEA and its standards in later chapters.)

Over the next two years, the second and third progressive levels were introduced for years twelve and thirteen (K11–K12). The academic challenge of these levels was restored to that of before NCEA, whilst retaining the flexibility to design courses to best suit the students within a school. That might sound straightforward enough, but there were problems in modifying the ingrained educational culture amongst the teachers. As you can imagine, changing the way 50,000 teachers assessed and operated did not succeed overnight. The high school teachers who were charged with presenting this new approach to students had developed their pedagogy in the twentieth century, and it included a high dose of standardised testing.

Complicating matters was the fact that the residing culture within education had developed before access to the Internet and mobile technology. Amidst the overhaul of an entrenched system, New Zealand's teachers (along with the rest of the world's educators) had to come to terms with young people's sudden access to the Internet. Many educators still viewed themselves as part of an important information delivery system. The new, more flexible assessment system was capable of dealing with (and maximising on) the advantages technology offered, but changing the habits of teachers in their classrooms would take time.

Viewing NCEA from the perspective of a teacher, generations had become used to exam-based assessment. It was tempting to develop a traditional set of teaching material for each NCEA standard and then create a standardised test for all the students. In many cases, this is exactly what happened. The evolution of New Zealand education required an insistent push to move high school teachers away from writing tests (more on that later).

In 2000, educators, business leaders, and government representatives conducted the initial review of the country's curriculum, looking for ways where it needed to better match changing world trends. The review included public consultations that led to thousands of ideas on how to improve *what* and *how* students learned. By 2007, five years into NCEA assessment, the final (and still current) version of the new curriculum was published to all schools. The surprise for many, including teachers who had not chosen to get involved in the development of the new document, was that the new curriculum essentially contained no content to deliver to students! It was less a list of things to deliver and more a framework for developing young people as confident, twenty-first-century learners. A key difference for me, coming from the United Kingdom, was that the new curriculum concerned the learner more than the content. The document's foreword stated, *"It takes as its starting point a vision of our young people as lifelong learners who are confident and creative, connected, and actively involved."*[5] So let's take a closer look at what a learner-focused, almost content-free curriculum looks like.

---

5 "The New Zealand Curriculum Online." 2009. 17 Dec. 2015, http://nzcurriculum.tki.org.nz/The-New-Zealand-Curriculum

Questions for Readers

1. What efforts or results indicate that your country's education reflects the times in which we live?

2. Is your education system separate enough from politics to allow it to develop without interference every four years?

3. To what extent is your elementary schooling defined by the demands of high school assessment?

The 'Empty' New Zealand Curriculum

One of my favourite paragraphs in the current New Zealand national curriculum appears even before the first page of the document's content. On the inside of the cover, the Ministry of Education explains why the document uses the nautilus as its metaphoric emblem:

> *Physician, writer, and poet Oliver Wendell Holmes (1809–94) saw the spiral shell of the nautilus as a symbol of intellectual and spiritual growth. He suggested that people outgrew their protective shells and discarded them as they became no longer necessary: "One's mind, once stretched by a new idea, never regains its original dimensions."[6] (New Zealand Curriculum p.2)*

I have never heard a better description of what education is all about than to outgrow one's protective shell—to stretch oneself and be stretched by new ideas. The document relates an understanding of

---

6 "The New Zealand Curriculum Online." 2009. 17 Dec. 2015, http://nzcurriculum.tki.org.nz/The-New-Zealand-Curriculum

our rapidly changing world that is constantly developing culturally and technologically. Because of this understanding, it does not contain absolute statements about what specific content schools should be teaching. Instead, the emphasis is on twenty-first-century values and competencies, as it states in its foreword:

> *It sets out values that are to be encouraged, modelled, and explored. It defines five key competencies that are critical to sustained learning and effective participation in society and that underline the emphasis on lifelong learning. (New Zealand Curriculum p.6)*

The document contains thirty-nine pages of content, only twelve of which are dedicated to what you might call traditional curriculum content. Even then, those twelve don't mention any actual content and, instead, only explain key competencies within each of the eight learning areas:

- English
- The Arts
- Health and Physical Education
- Learning Languages
- Mathematics and Statistics
- Science
- Social Sciences
- Technology

The curriculum document sets an example by not including any specific content to be delivered. It was, after all, created to be viewed as a framework for educators. The foreword continues:

> *The challenge now is to build on this framework, offering our young people the most effective and engaging teaching possible and supporting them to achieve to the highest of standards. (New Zealand Curriculum p.4)*

It notes that schools are expected to be working towards personalisation of learning experiences:

> When designing and reviewing their curriculum, schools select achievement objectives from each area in response to the identified interests and learning needs of their students. (New Zealand Curriculum p.44)

By comparison, the UK curriculum updated in 2014 offers a far more prescriptive model ("these items must be taught to students"), based on twentieth-century delivery methods. The United Kingdom's high school curriculum description is literally ten times the length of the New Zealand equivalent. In the United States, the exhaustive lists of skills, content, and suggested texts contained in the Common Core standards encourage a similar teacher-driven environment. It's an approach that leaves little room for students to personalise their learning.

As an example, the New Zealand Curriculum has less than a page of objectives each for both English and math. It also introduces the learning areas with this statement:

> While the learning areas are presented as distinct, **this should not limit the ways in which schools structure the learning experiences offered to students.** (New Zealand Curriculum p.18)

The aim is that schools will develop their own curriculum from the framework. This is a key example of the level of trust the government administrators have placed in the educators to decide what's best for young people in different parts of the country.

What's in an "Empty" Curriculum?

The first half of the document is dedicated to the general values, competencies, and principles centred on young people developing as confident, connected world citizens. In my travels around the country visiting schools, I can report that New Zealand educators are genuinely dedicated to promoting these values and competencies. Not trapped by a prescriptive set of topics, teachers are free to focus on the life skills important to developing lifelong learners.

The vision for young people as laid out by the curriculum emphasises focus on the character traits listed below rather than subject mastery.

- Confidence
- Connection
- Active involvement in a range of contexts
- A Commitment to Lifelong Learning[7]

Likewise, its values focus on developing qualities including the following:

- Excellence
- Innovation, inquiry, and curiosity
- Diversity
- Equity
- Community and participation
- Ecological sustainability
- Integrity
- Respect for self, others, and human rights

The key competencies prioritised in New Zealand's curriculum document:

- Thinking
- Relating to others
- Using language, symbols, and texts
- Managing self
- Participating and contributing

---

7 "The New Zealand Curriculum - NZ Curriculum Online - TKI." 2009. 25 May 2016, http://nzcurriculum.tki.org.nz/The-New-Zealand-Curriculum

Now, these values and key competencies are common in many countries' curriculum documents. The difference in New Zealand is that we don't then go on to drown them out with prescribed lists of compulsory topics. This is what allows teachers to stay focused on the values, character traits, and competencies that prepare young people for a rapidly developing world. What's so powerful about New Zealand's approach is the combination of trusting educators to make sense of these brief priority statements *without* prescribing exact content, style of delivery, or assessment. The curriculum is written to create a live and developing education community rather than the kind of top-down, "you must" culture that has produced negative outcomes in many countries.

Issues with Specifying Compulsory Topics

I'm going to use the subject of history for this one, as it often "suffers" in other countries from higher authorities prescribing topic lists. An example from the UK Secondary Curriculum that worries me is that *all children* must be taught "the development of church, state, and society in medieval Britain 1066–1509" (UK Secondary Curriculum p.96). The idea that the development of the church in medieval Britain should be relevant to every child in the United Kingdom, regardless of circumstance, seems as bizarre to me now as a teacher as it did when I was a student. For me, the compulsory specification pushes schools away from the idea that an individual learner's needs and interests have any relevance. And what about the great year of 1510? It doesn't even get a foot in the door!

I'm not saying history or any particular study is not important. What I am highlighting is that New Zealand allows schools, teachers, and, most importantly, students to tailor the focus of historical study, with the aim of developing a personal intrinsic motivation to master the skills and processes necessary for discovering good sources and analysing the evidence. Personal interest makes the learning relevant and is likely to strengthen the future of historical study and understanding. If we want more historians in the world, we need a generation of deep thinkers who are driven by genuine connections to what interests them. The focus on teaching student discovery skills, rather than focusing primarily on facts and dates, also encourages teachers to move on from what they may have previously used as content. In the New Zealand schools I have worked with, fewer teachers are peddling the same material year to year. The expectation within the teaching community is for improvement on previous learning experiences. This expectation for continual development (rather than teaching stagnation) is monitored through our practising certification system. Our system in New Zealand has a set of systematic checks in place, including compulsory requirements, to network and moderate between teachers and schools. This means that a teacher of history can be expected and trusted to work with other history teachers to develop, refine, and keep the history curriculum relevant for their respective schools. This includes personalising it to local and community interests where appropriate. The practising certification system checks and confirms each teacher's professional development every three years, something I cover later on in the book in chapter nine.

In addition to forcing rote, impersonal learning, prescribed, top-down curriculums promote a lack of faith in the educators' ability to choose what's best for their students at the time the learning takes place. Such prescriptions allow little room to contextualise the learning to make it seem relevant. This lack of faith seeps into the wider society, significantly diminishing the status of teachers as professionals.

In the New Zealand Curriculum, there is less focus on telling teachers what to teach and more advice on developing better pedagogy. A fantastic observation I made of this framework is that its objectives for effective pedagogy take up three times the page space of any learning area (subject).

Benefits of School Autonomy

What does it look like when all public schools are autonomous from the government in all essential matters to make decisions around curriculum, subjects, staffing, timetabling, learning approaches, and extra-curricular activities? There are many benefits to school autonomy, and I will take you through the academic issues in later chapters. Here, I would like to highlight how autonomous schools can directly benefit students' personal cultural awareness and tolerance.

New Zealand, and especially Auckland, is extremely multicultural. I've been to two schools that have displays of all the flags representing the nationalities held by their student populations. In both cases, there were more than forty countries represented! However, like any place on the earth, each culture often gravitates towards particular suburbs, making the cohort of students in one public school culturally different from another. School autonomy means that leaders and teachers are free to build learning environments based on the cultural experiences and specific understandings held by the community. This makes the educational experience much more meaningful and personal, whilst still delivering the skills and knowledge areas outlined in the curriculum.

As an example of this personalisation, my wife, a high school health teacher, was able to take the topical New Zealand issue of Pacific Islanders' specific problems with type 2 diabetes and allow any of her students to carry out a study for part of their high school graduation on members of their own family. The learning felt authentic. The fact that the study was for assessment was a non-issue for the students.

Autonomous Schools Mean
Responsive Education

Autonomy also allows for responsive schools, better able to reflect the rapidly changing opportunities available to each school generation. A school generation is something that I see as roughly a decade. The new opportunities and technologies that have appeared during the past three decades have been a constant reminder that education must promote adaptability through the way it operates. Yet most national systems have been designed and have operated in such a way as to not allow schools to reflect truly what was going on in the world.

As long as most developed countries continue to prescribe the content to be delivered in every school, we cannot say that the world of education is responsive to individual learners' needs. We live in a world where people are expected to demonstrate their own unique skillsets. It seems, then, that the world's nations should ensure their systems of education employ the kind of personalisation that allows students to practise developing the skillsets they might offer the world.

Are There Any Rules?

Obviously, every school is still held to account for following the national curriculum framework. There has to be evidence within a school of the curriculum's vision, values, and key competencies. These are checked regularly (every two to five years) by the government's Education Review Office (ERO). Schools must also follow national education guidelines[8] and national administrative guidelines.[9] But most importantly, schools are held to account for creating learning environments that develop confident, connected, actively involved learners and citizens.

---

8 "The National Education Guidelines (NEGs) | Education in New Zealand." 2014. 10 May 2016, http://www.education.govt.nz/ministry-of-education/legislation/the-national-education-guidelines/
9 "The National Administration Guidelines (NAGs) - Ministry of Education." 2015. 10 May 2016, http://www.education.govt.nz/ministry-of-education/legislation/nags/

Questions for Readers

1. Who decides what topics or content should be in your school curriculum?

2. Why is any one topic relevant to all learners in a country?

3. How does your national educational structure reflect a world of personalisation?

Chapter 3
A High-Trust Model

Education by Educators? What a crazy idea!

It seems obvious that education should be designed and operated by educators. After all, we trust that doctors know what they're doing. We assume most judges and lawyers are capable of making decisions about the law. So why do so many teachers around the world feel trapped in systems over which they have no control?

This lack of control particularly causes strife when teachers want to—or are asked to—apply "modern" approaches to learning. Whether you're reading this in the United Kingdom, the United States, or in any number of countries where what is taught is decided by a higher authority, you may be curious about how education works when teachers are trusted to choose exactly what, when, and how to learn with their students. I use the word *learn* in the previous sentence quite consciously. A curriculum that does not state topics also does the very important job of promoting learning as an ongoing process rather than a fixed-term, predetermined experience that is somehow over when you complete your school exams. New Zealand's curriculum dedicates pages to how teachers should best maintain their own learning in an inquiry and collaborative model. The way it is written, our curriculum pushes teachers to model learning for students because doing so is one of the most effective ways to encourage lifelong learning in young people.

New Zealand Expects Connected Educators

Was social media the true birth of the teaching profession? Let's look at a brief history:

One aspect of twenty-first-century teaching, with which an educator-empowered system nicely dovetails, is the worldwide emphasis on being connected. This expectation that teachers would network and learn from others in their field is relatively new. I like to compare education with the legal and medical professions with an aim of highlighting how educators can use technology tools, like social media, to rebuild the sense that we are part of a global profession. The legal and medical professions have been expected to—and some might say *paid* to—maintain an effective network. In 2002, when I trained to be a teacher in the United Kingdom, we were essentially presented with the idea that a teacher must choose to practise one of several educational theories. It was a closed model of personal choice and, at the end of the day, a teacher was left isolated in his classroom to deliver the best he could. With a predetermined curriculum that left little room for creative thinking, behavioural issues were the teacher's main professional concern.

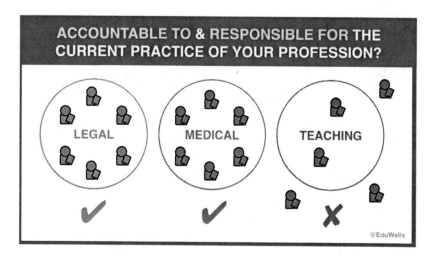

The idea that educators were part of a global profession, a support system from which we could all benefit, never entered my mind until about 2006. Why 2006? Because that was the year many of us were introduced to Ken Robinson when he presented a TED Talk that inspired millions of educators. A teacher in my school at the time decided to open a meeting with an eighteen-minute video of Ken's talk. It was quite a special moment for everyone in the room. Now, the reason I mention Ken is not because I think he has the answer to everything, but because he has since been interviewed and stated that he, too, was taken aback by the sudden explosion in interest focused on him and his talk. He, and most educators at the time, had yet to realise the power social media had to connect professionals. Social media was quite new, and up to that point, most of us used it to stay in touch with friends and family members.

The evolution of social media brought about a significant shift in the teaching profession, suddenly making it a single, connected entity in its own right. The early adopters within this new connected world were the first to set up social media accounts as educators rather than for personal reasons. Three years later, Shelly Sanchez Terrell (@ShellTerrell), Tom Whitby (@TomWhitby), and Steven Anderson (@Web20classroom) founded #EdChat when they realised the power of hashtags to collate conversation and resources on Twitter.

How Do You Use Social Media?

To illustrate what I mean by early adopters, I include here my representation of the very well-shared "Pencil Metaphor" for integrating technology or, in fact, any educational idea in schools. Have a look and decide where you'd place yourself.

As I write this, #EdChat is six years old and is now complemented by hundreds of chats that specialise in every educational area and topic in need of debate. #EdTech for technology use, #SciChat and #MathChat for Science and Math respectively. If you search online for "educational hashtags," you'll discover a long list of chats from which you can choose the ones that suit your interests.

This isn't a book about the workings of social media for teachers, so if you need an introduction to professional use of hashtags, etc., I will point you to the excellent summary by Edudemic.[1]

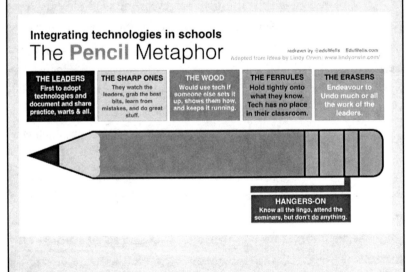

Integrating technologies in schools
The **Pencil** Metaphor

redrawn by @eduWells EduWells.com
Adapted from ideas by Lindy Orwin: www.lindyorwin.com/

THE LEADERS	THE SHARP ONES	THE WOOD	THE FERRULES	THE ERASERS
First to adopt technologies and document and share practice, warts & all.	They watch the leaders, grab the best bits, learn from mistakes, and do great stuff.	Would use tech if someone else sets it up, shows them how, and keeps it running.	Hold tightly onto what they know. Tech has no place in their classroom.	Endeavour to Undo much or all the work of the leaders.

HANGERS-ON
Know all the lingo, attend the seminars, but don't do anything.

1   "The Teacher's Guide to Twitter, Edudemic, 2013. 10 May 2016, http://www.edudemic.com/guides/guide-to-twitter/

Teaching as Inquiry

The topic of professional development can spark conversations that go on for hours. (Trust me, I've sat through hundreds of planning meetings.) You can spend one meeting after the next discussing how to approach professional development as a school: Who needs what? Should there be elements of compulsory training? And the most frightening and misguided question, *Which tech should we be using?* In all the schools I worked in during the first decade of my teaching career, these marathon meetings led to minimal success.

Even today, many teachers' vision for how learning should look is based on their own school experiences. Some see professional development as a sporadic series of (often-disappointing) events that they choose to or are asked to attend. What is most sad to me is when I meet student-centred teachers who, when providing training to other staff, do not use their normal classroom techniques because they know the audience of teachers are expecting and comfortable with the stand-and-deliver format. It is certainly not a bad thing that the number of education conferences continues to grow. But the attendees at these events tend to be from the minority of teachers who have developed some type of growth mindset. The majority of teachers I've worked within schools, both in the UK and here in New Zealand, have yet to attend such an event, and many wouldn't see much need to. Remember, the New Zealand system is fantastic, but Kiwi teachers are still coming to terms with it.

The question for any education system, then, is this: How do we make having a growth mindset the norm amongst educators? In truth, it takes time to develop a culture where growth is the expectation, but including a systematic approach to developing this mindset as part of your national curriculum document is a good first step.

A National Growth Mindset

It is with great pleasure I can tell you that New Zealand is systematically solving the issue of nationwide, authentic professional development. The solution comes from making every teacher accountable for designing and reporting a personal inquiry into their own classroom practice. This is done through an action research model we call *Teaching as Inquiry* (TAI). Asking teachers to challenge and reflect upon their teaching automatically makes it more relevant and personal than if they were following a mandated lesson plan—or even simply following their own lesson plans from the previous year. This call for continual personal reflection and professional development is the opposite of any form of one-size-fits-all approach. The trick is to make teachers accountable for sharing their reflections with, at a minimum, others in their school and, more preferably, the world. The style of learning and area of growth targeted are chosen by each individual teacher and are expected to produce a measurable challenge to some aspect of their teaching.

The purpose of TAI is to instil in teachers the belief that professional development is, and should be, instigated by the individual. It also promotes the idea that development and learning is continuous and not isolated to planned events. The best professional development comes from reflecting on one's own practice and applying measurable challenges to one's own teaching. It is a practice that empowers teach-

The best professional development comes from reflecting on one's own practice and applying measurable challenges to one's own teaching.

ers to keep and improve the good stuff whilst throwing out the things that don't make a measurable difference to learning in their classroom or school. Teachers are then encouraged to share those measurable challenges or inquiries with other educators, be it in one-to-one meetings with a "critical" friend or on a blog, as a growing number of Kiwi teachers now do. TAI is a practice that is successfully developing a culture amongst teachers in New Zealand for collaborative reflection and shared growth. This culture, in turn, helps to build trust within the system as teachers are more accountable and transparent in what they are doing and trying to achieve. The sharing of TAIs also provides a library of ideas and resources to any educator willing to tap into the blogs and wikis created by their fellow educators.

I created this diagram of the SITTI model[2] to show how the TAI process fits with schools' professional development goals and creates a vision for learning that includes everyone.

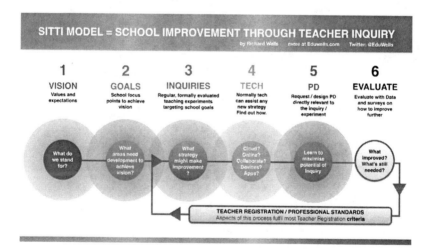

SITTI MODEL = SCHOOL IMPROVEMENT THROUGH TEACHER INQUIRY
by Richard Wells   more at Eduwells.com   Twitter: @EduWells

1	2	3	4	5	6
VISION	GOALS	INQUIRIES	TECH	PD	EVALUATE
Values and expectations	School focus points to achieve vision	Regular, formally evaluated teaching experiments targeting school goals	Normally tech can assist any new strategy Find out how.	Request / design PD directly relevant to the inquiry / experiment	Evaluate with Data and surveys on how to improve further

What do we stand for? — What areas need development to achieve vision? — What strategy might make improvement? — Cloud? Online? Collaborate? Devices? Apps? — Learn to maximise potential of Inquiry — What improved? What's still needed?

TEACHER REGISTRATION / PROFESSIONAL STANDARDS
Aspects of this process fulfil most Teacher Registration criteria

---

2   "SITTI – School Improvement Through Teacher Inquiry..."
2015. 9 Apr. 2016, http://eduwells.com/2014/10/26/
sitti-school-improvement-through-teacher-inquiry/

Questions for Readers

1. In what ways are your country's educators trusted as professionals or directed by administrators?

2. Should a school lead a community in education, or vice-versa?

3. What initiatives does your country run in order to build respect for teachers and reassurance for the public to trust educators?

Chapter 4

What It Means to Be a New Zealand Teacher

What does all this look like when a New Zealand teacher turns up for work at the beginning of a school year?

I thought it would be informative to take you through the New Zealand educator's year. That way I can highlight the important moments and quality checks that take place within this educator-run system. We divide the year into four equal terms of ten weeks, with a two-week break between them. What I've written here is not a minute-by-minute account, but it explains some of the issues New Zealand's teachers deal with in each quarter of the school year. I'll try to cover the thoughts and priorities that might be unique to New Zealand teachers.

Before School Starts—New Ideas

The challenge during the summer for many New Zealand teachers, who fully control the education they provide, is curating and designing learning experiences from the sometimes multiple new ideas they have for the next twelve months, including approaches to assessment. Not all New Zealand teachers are up to speed with all of the initiatives in this book, but the ones who are will have challenged much of their previous twelve month's teaching practice. They'll be planning to refocus the students towards new themes and/or more relevant and topical information. An increasing number of teachers plan whole new approaches to learning each year and reevaluate how to involve students in the decisions about what happens in the classroom.

Term One: February–April

Inquiry for All

The school year in New Zealand begins in the first week of February. Typically, schools start the year with the traditional and still-practised Māori welcoming ceremony that introduces all parties to the school, especially the new students and teachers. (Search YouTube for "school pōwhiri" to see these school-opening ceremonies.)

In high schools, the initial two weeks of teacher meetings are spent analysing the last year's results and discussing minor changes to units and/or planning for major redesigns for standards to be covered later in the year. Any significant new projects require moderation to make sure they align to the national standards and assessments. During this time, educators plan their own *Teaching as Inquiry (TAI)* research project and often share these plans for improvement with colleagues. "How am I challenging my practice this year?" is the question New Zealand teachers are expected to ask.

In most high schools (K10–12), teachers meet in February to complete plans for high school assessment for the year. This planning actually begins during final stages of the previous year, but remains open to tweaking if the teachers in a school feel the proposed projects might be made more relevant, given current events or opportunities for cross-curricular assessment. Educators then develop and moderate the guidance material the students will use to ensure they earn credits for their work to graduate from high school. It is a requirement that the material clearly indicates, with examples, how a student would display excellence-level thinking and understanding for each topic. As I mentioned before, this process of constructing assessment each year is becoming an increasingly collaborative effort between the teacher and the students themselves. Whatever format the students' projects take, the moderation between educators of the guidance material continues throughout the year. This quality assurance check simply has to be done before anything is officially started. But notice again, the educators are trusted to do this as a profession. The standards-based approach has also started encouraging a growing number of schools to use cross-curricular projects that require combinations of skills and knowledge across multiple traditional disciplines, which can then add to one's high school graduation.

At the elementary and middle school level, teachers start their year by finalising the themes for student study that they will use to divide the year. They are also expected to align the potential outcomes of any students' inquiry projects to the eight learning areas within the curriculum.[1] Many schools aim some of these inquiries at local or national initiatives. Our primary television channel has held a number of national competitions around successful student projects. My next-door neighbour, an eleven-year-old girl, actually won a competition with her two school friends by producing a documentary on battery farming.

---

1   The eight learning areas are English, the arts, health and physical education, learning languages, mathematics and statistics, science, social sciences, and technology.

In recent years, the initial planning that occurs in the first term has begun to include students at all age levels. Elementary and middle school students now hold negotiation meetings with their teachers to plan their own inquiries (leaning) for the year. The schools that are leading the change in New Zealand are now discussing how senior students might plan and design their own high school graduation assessments for the year. This means the students would not simply be choosing school subjects but would have the ability to develop large projects where skills, competencies, and knowledge can be aligned with relevant graduation standards. The intention of this shift is to ensure that the qualification is obtained as a byproduct of the students' work rather than as the sole focus of it.

Term Two: May–July

An example of the quality checking that takes place in this educator- and student-driven system is when samples of high school graduation work that were sent off to national moderators in the previous year are returned to schools. (Moderators are teachers who volunteer for training and funding to check marks.) The returned work contains reports on grade judgments that were made by teachers within the school. In many schools, this occurs during the second term, but the process is ongoing throughout the year. Groups of subject specialist high school teachers will have sent off samples of work at each achievement level, and the report explains how much these grade decisions align with those given nationally. At this point, the teachers in the school are expected to make adjustments, hopefully minor, to their future assessment matrix. This can involve further meetings with individual students to ensure their projects meet national expectations for each topic standard. As an example, I have received back moderation reports suggesting students provide more evidence of how they worked with independence and economised their use of time and resources. This led us to encourage blogging and reflections alongside the assessed project.

Here's one result of this blogging as an example.[2]

Some further information needs be provided about how the students worked with independence and accuracy for merit and economy for excellence.

Term Two is also the start of new inquiry themes in many elementary/primary schools. Alongside personal inquiries on which elementary students work, most schools will choose termly themes for all students in which to inquire. Some schools allow students to tackle these themes individually, whilst other schools design inquiries for the class to do as a whole. My daughters have carried out school inquiries on themes such as ecology, music industry, and astronomy. The approach taken is inquiry based because they know they are preparing students for a future high school experience where they'll be increasingly involved in shaping both their school work and format of assessment.

Term Three: July–September

The beginning of each term in most elementary and middle schools will normally start new themes for student inquiry projects. A funny observation I've noticed in my house is that being able to shape their student-driven inquiry means it infiltrates all their normal habits. My eight-year-old rushed in the other day, excited to have found a show on Netflix about planets—her current school theme—and had decided to find all the requirements for setting up home on Jupiter. I explained this might be difficult, but she said, "It's a bigger planet with more to see, and we just need to make our house strong enough." I thought this was excellent, as it would lead her to discover why this wasn't feasible, driven by curiosity rather than teacher request. I've observed, too, that being in charge of one's learning also means that planning or reshaping projects also happens amongst the text messages between young people.

---

2   https://christhompson23896.wordpress.com/page/2/

Throughout the high school year, but especially during the third term, teachers mentor students and review the states of their various projects. We highlight where more evidence is needed to achieve better grades and show excellence-level thinking on each topic standard. Since much of our high school students' work is required to be stored or published online, it is during this term that students and teachers collate and/or confirm the URLs to all the evidence that will be graded.

I want to point out here that some schools will still be running exam preparation and practice during the third term. Although our schools and educators can work with autonomy, New Zealand hasn't completely escaped standardised testing yet. The nature of the education system New Zealand is developing is working well to move educators away from standardised testing; however, some schools and teachers continue to choose to use it. The difference is that the testing is a choice teachers can make; it is not a mandated practice.

Term Four: October–December

In high schools, the beginning of Term Four is a time to complete larger projects, be they single subject or cross curricular. Multi-standard projects, such as my school's product development tasks, are graded by each teacher by combining the marking matrix for each NCEA standard being assessed. For example, our product development includes standards on developing a design brief, consulting with stakeholders, and developing prototypes. Grades are moderated by educators, normally within the same school, to ensure marking judgements align; sample packs will be prepared in the event that the ministry requires the grades to be assessed by the national moderation team.

It's Not All Good News

As I mentioned earlier, Term Four does still include exams in some schools. Students who have earned enough credits for qualifications and graduation through their projects throughout the school year may choose not to take any formal standardised exams, avoiding them altogether.

I mentioned early on in this book that school culture is often governed by the next educational stage, which is why improving the high school assessment has had a positive effect on the learning experience in younger grades. Unfortunately for our high school students, universities continue to give hours of standardised exams. As a result, genuine transformation to something truly meaningful in education is cut short. Rather than fully embracing the possibilities that autonomy could create, many high school teachers feel constrained by the conviction that they must prepare their students for the kind of testing they will endure at the university level. As an example of this frightening circumstance, a science teacher told me that his school's department felt hamstrung by the local university, which had taken to dictating which NCEA science standards it wanted future students to have achieved. These were all standardised tests, as the university felt this was the best indicator for who would succeed in their establishment. The university in question is now showing signs of modernising, with flipped teaching, etc., and the science teacher is hoping this will flow on to reviews of their assessment practice. But for now, he remains constrained to keep the university happy.

For me, there's nothing worse than seeing educators exist in a purely academic bubble, disconnected from the changes in the world, dictating a one-size-fits-all format for learning. Personalised, student-centred learning[3] will do far more to prepare students for their future than any standardised test.

---

3   "What is Student-Centred Learning? – @EDUWELLS." 2016. 9 Apr. 2016, http://eduwells.com/2016/03/05/what-is-student-centred-learning/

Questions for Readers

1. How are teachers in your country influencing the improvement of the national education system?

2. In a personalised world, how is standardised testing being rationalised in your part of the educational system?

3. What evidence do you have that your education system formally recognises world trends and developments?

Chapter 5
Connected New Zealand

New Zealand's
Communities of Schools

I f you are a teacher, do you know what your students did in school before they came to your class? If you are like many teachers I've spoken with throughout my career, your answer is probably no. In fact, many teachers know nothing of what students have done in previous schools before arriving in their classrooms. I would even go so far as to say that the culture of education sets the expectation that teachers should build classes from scratch every year. I have also heard many stories of university lecturers joking with their undergraduates about forgetting all they learnt in school because the "real" education starts with them.

Not knowing (or, worse, not caring) what your students learnt before they walked through your classroom's door indicates a lack of interest in what each stage of education offers students. One issue in this area that occasionally pops up in conversation is teachers' assumption that students have little to learn from teachers of younger age groups.[1] High school teachers, in particular, show negligible genuine interest in anything that happens in middle or elementary schools. Every year, I have conversations with teachers who openly indicate their ignorance in regard to what younger children do at school and the approach to learning taken by schools that come before them. The shame in this is that as educators around the world become more connected, the technology and pedagogies used during early childhood and elementary teaching develop at surprising rates. When teachers of older children remain ignorant of these developments, they underestimate the progress made by students in the earlier years. This can lead to inappropriately reduced expectations of students in high schools.

The disconnect and lack of collaboration between schools has a cumulative negative effect. Firstly, little is done to make a learner's transition through the system a seamless process that makes the most of each stage. Secondly, I have observed from conversations with teachers throughout the country that the oldest students in each school, including kindergarten, are expected to lead, be responsible for things, and even make decisions for others.[2] Those same children then move on to their next school and, even though they are a year older, as the youngest in their new school, they are treated as incapable and needy. In many cases, the expectation to lead situations in their learning is removed entirely and much potential is lost.

---

1   "What Every School Can Learn From Preschools : NPR Ed : NPR." 2015. 11 May 2016, http://www.npr.org/sections/ed/2014/11/25/366561443/what-every-school-can-learn-from-preschools

2   "School Transitions – Kings and Queens reduced to Pawns - eduwells." 2016. 11 May 2016, https://eduwells.com/2015/08/29/school-transitions-kings-and-queens-reduced-to-pawns/

I visited a kindergarten in 2015 that has a leadership programme for their four-year-olds. The teachers met with students and discussed what leaders do and say. They introduced the leaders on the classroom wall with photos and leadership statements, such as four-year-old Eva highlighting, "When you're being a leader, you can't scratch, and you use kind words." Aiden, also four, discussed setting an example: "You put the blocks back where they should go, so that others can see where they go." The children were expected to help make decisions about the school's initiatives. Having two daughters myself and having visited many elementary schools, I was fully aware that the "normal" teaching approach for first grade classes was to have students sit on a floor mat and do all the same activities. This school's approach was impressively far from "normal."

In 2014, New Zealand's Ministry of Education launched a new nationwide programme called "Communities of Learning" to fund and support the connection and collaboration of schools within a region. The programme's aim was to create consistent pathways for students through their education and thus raise achievement. And although the programme's funding comes from central government, it is run and operated purely by teachers. A principal oversees a group of teachers who receive time and funding to organise collaborative projects and establish information channels between schools to ensure that a student's transition from one school to the next is successful.

These new communication channels between schools have helped to clear up issues caused by different expectations applied to young people as they move into a new school. Additionally, teachers are becoming more aware of what each stage offers and how the various approaches to learning can be built upon rather than discarded. More collaboration between schools supports the belief that educators comprise a single profession and are not simply a collection of isolated schools and teachers just doing a job. The initiative of this connected community of schools dovetails nicely with the TAI and collaborative planning and evaluating measures to further develop a national growth mindset through the positive promotion of collaboration. Over the next few years, I look forward to seeing direct evidence of students both benefitting from and becoming aware of this collaboration as they build a view of their own learning as a continuous experience of personal growth, rather than isolated learning events and institutions. I have said for years that the Internet, and especially social media, gives every individual inspired to make a difference the power to do so. If the Communities of Learning concept embeds and those kindergarten kids I met last year are allowed to build on their leadership experiences, just imagine how confident and successful they might be before even leaving formal education.

The Pond—Resource Sharing Nationally

Talking to educators around the world, the common approach taken by many governments and administrations is based on a control model. It is normally the government that centrally envisions what is best for teachers to deliver to the nation's youth. This is certainly the case in the United States and the United Kingdom. In this country, the government's connection to its own education system is primarily built on respect for educators' ability to develop what's best for their learners. I have already provided plenty of evidence for this truth, but to show you how the government also endorses the collaborative approach to education development, I need to introduce you to "The Pond." This initiative was a joint venture between the ministry and private enterprise to provide an open collaborative environment for New Zealand teachers to connect and share teaching ideas and resources. Based on the Creative Commons objectives, teachers can sign up and help to fuel education with their ideas and resources. In many cases, these resources help to deepen the thinking of teachers because of an increased awareness of best practices.

KidsEdChatNZ

When I first think of globally connected classrooms, I immediately think of systems such as Skype Classroom, Quad-blogging or Google's Connected Classrooms. But to me, the important point around global student discussion—or, in fact, any situation that introduces new perspectives to a classroom topic—is the depth of *messy learning*.

ACHIEVING SUCCESS

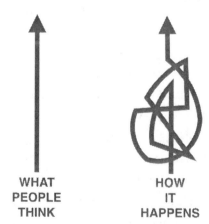

WHAT PEOPLE THINK

HOW IT HAPPENS

This is my rendition of an image created by Demetri Martin that very accurately depicts the true path of success.

You may have seen an image like the one on the previous page depicting success. Well, I like to think the same about learning. It is detrimental to education when anything or any person encourages the idea that learning occurs on a straight path from point A to point B. The linear learning idea is established in the belief that, at the beginning of learning, you don't know something, but after following a particular study path, you complete your learning by obtaining said knowledge. True, deep learning is a social exercise. Multiple perspectives are always required if a genuine understanding is to be achieved. Even your own perspectives may not become apparent to you unless or until you involve other people in the conversation.

The teachers who understand the importance of connecting students and classrooms to the world for new perspectives typically have at least three driving questions:

- How young can we start this process?
- How best can we showcase positive and relevant online behaviour?
- If we start young, how do we ensure safety?

This is where I would like to introduce you to a Kiwi named Stephen Baker (@PalmyTeacher). For two years, Stephen and his small team of volunteer teachers have run a hugely successful classroom Twitter chat every Wednesday afternoon. When I say successful, I mean that more than 230 elementary classrooms have been involved; and remember, New Zealand only has a population of four million! The chat can be found on Twitter using the #KidsEdChatNZ hashtag or @KidsEdChatNZ. It also has a website.[3]

Every week, one of the team members posts the questions for participating classes to answer on Wednesday, between two and three in the afternoon. The classroom accounts are added to a Twitter list, which they then subscribe to in order to isolate the discussion from the rest of Twitter. Students respond to one another's reflections and thoughts.

---

3   http://kidsedchatnz.blogspot.co.nz

Past questions have included a range of topics:
- What does good problem-solving look like?
- Should you be able to use Minecraft in your school/classroom? Convince us! How can it help learning?
- How do your school's values impact your learning?
- Can you think of any problems that you could solve with coding?

Although this is a national initiative, #KidsEdChat has introduced thousands of children, as young as five, to a world of online connections and to the learning those connections bring about. They also get to see online discussion in the context of a real social media platform safely monitored by the classroom teacher.

Why not a #KidsEdChatGlobal? To have students discuss their learning and reflect on one another's perspectives could have similar positive outcomes to our homegrown equivalent. The question is, will you be the teacher to start it?

The Mind Lab by Unitec

Although this book is targeted at explaining the joys of a quality public education system, I want to note that some private initiatives also shine New Zealand in very good light. We are lucky to have an inspirational leader in New Zealand named Frances Valintine, who founded the nonprofit enterprise, The Mind Lab. In conjunction with a public university, The Mind Lab offers teachers a single-year course on future-focused pedagogies and technologies. The organisation's primary goal is to inspire thousands of teachers to develop growth mindsets and gain recognised postgraduate qualifications by taking an in-depth study of these new practices.

I was lucky enough to go through this course, where I heard Valintine point out that education was dangerously falling behind many other aspects of life, such as business and medicine, in the way it operated and interacted with the world. She noted that educators were not keeping pace with the world's rapid rate of change, a reality that was not good for preparing young people for current and future developments.

As a nonprofit, The Mind Lab receives public money and offers more than 2,000 teachers free scholarships to attend and complete the course. Within two years of its inception, The Mind Lab by Unitec grew from one to four centres, and thousands of teachers had completed the programme. The outgrowth of the initiative is the impact these teachers are now having in their schools, where they pass on the information and training to colleagues within their schools. From what I've seen, this is perhaps a more powerful way to learn than listening to an external professional-development provider deliver similar content.

As an example of the type of topics studied at The Mind Lab, it was there that I was introduced to design thinking. Design thinking is an excellent model for education in general, as it has a bias towards both action and building empathy for how humans are affected by any topic being studied. Teachers of all subjects use design thinking, and I've seen it used from grades four to twelve. Rather than add all the details here, I've written a post on what I learned about design thinking[4] at The Mind Lab. Here's a summary of the steps taken, often timed segments to encourage progress, to build a solution and/or product with design thinking:

1. Take time for silent thinking to collect any thoughts individuals might have on the subject/problem. This improves any group work as it allows quieter personalities time to prepare their contribution, which can often be overshadowed by dominant personalities within the group.

2. Share ideas and collate. This is the stage normally seen as group work in classrooms.

3. Profile the lives of the target stakeholders. What, in their lives, might have an impact on our final proposal?

---

4 "Design Thinking in the Classroom – @EDUWELLS." 2016. 11 May 2016, https://eduwells.com/2015/02/04/design-thinking-in-the-classroom/

4. Empathise with stakeholders' current views and beliefs.

5. With whom do the stakeholders interact, and how might this impact the final solution or product?

6. Ideate and design.

7. Develop the prototype and/or pitch.

8. Groups pitch to each other.

9. Obtain feedback and improve the pitch for as many cycles as time allows.

Below is my quick infographic guide on the topic.

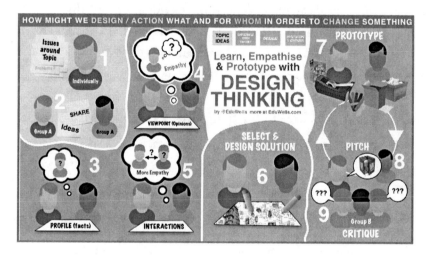

CORE Education NZ

In 2015, I was awarded a research fellowship to team up with six other top Kiwi teachers to help one another run personal inquiries into educational matters of interest. These projects studied issues such as identity development in early childhood education, design thinking in high schools, and community engagement in poor suburbs. I looked into if and how teachers were developing an awareness of their profession. And if they weren't, I asked, "Why not?" This excellent opportunity was arranged and funded by CORE Education, a non-profit agency that provides training and funds high-value research, ensuring the training and advice it offers remains at the cutting edge of global educational issues.

CORE Education is staffed by some of the most talented and intelligent educators I've met. The fellowship allowed us to spend time with a number of them, and each time we were shocked at how deeply thought provoking they could be in a relatively short session. You may have been to EdTech conferences and perhaps are involved in the online debate about the subject. Well, at CORE, they've moved well beyond the discussion of EdTech and live in a FutureEd bubble that's about ten years ahead of our time. It was CORE Education that took us on a tour of the leading New Zealand schools and inspired us all with amazing examples of how education could be very different and yield amazing outcomes.

CORE Education's ULearn Conference

New Zealand's biggest education conference is called Ulearn and is attended by approximately 2,000 educators from across the country. It does an excellent job of reflecting on how far New Zealand has come in comparison with other countries. For example, in 2006, the conference definitely had a focus on IT in education, but the event has since matured, and attendees now have expectations that the discussions will have a deeper focus around developing learners. Rather than still being focused on technology, most of the sessions are geared towards pedagogy, deep learning, and how twenty-first-century competencies are developed. Here are the questions that CORE Education asked attendees considering how to help them make the most of the conference:

- What is your school/inquiry focus, and what are your conference goals?
- In what ways are you planning to grow your professional practice?

- How does your school perceive student agency and what do "engaged learners" look like?
- How do you empower students as leaders of their own learning, and how do you measure the level of engagement?
- How is your school planning to create or utilise innovative learning spaces to maximum effect?
- Does your school have a focus on learning with digital technologies? What does this look like in action?
- Are you a school leader, and do you want to connect with other leaders and grow other leaders around you?
- Do you want to become more culturally responsive for Māori, Pasifika[5] students?
- Are you interested in learning design that is inclusive for all students?[6]

Notice how there's no talk of Google, Chromebooks, or iPads. Like everything else in New Zealand education, the aim is at growing and empowering learners and leaders to challenge numerous aspects of the status quo. Even someone like me, who reads and writes a lot about the cutting edge in world education trends, is challenged with new perspectives and new developments at this conference.

Parallel Connections Reach Deeper

I hope this chapter has given you a hint as to how connected New Zealand educators are. It's not just that we have various opportunities and initiatives, official or otherwise, but that they complement each other so nicely. The flexibility and teacher-led nature of the New Zealand system leads to a depth of discussion that is inspiring every time I find myself involved with these Kiwi education groups. It's these

---

5 New Zealand minority communities, targeted by the government as needing specific support and cultural understanding
6 "Programme - CORE events - CORE Education." 2013. 28 May 2016, http://www.events.core-ed.org/ulearn/programme

connected communities of educators that form parallel layers in a drive to extend the impact of New Zealand's unique education system. Connection with one group often leads to involvement with others. I hope I've encouraged more teachers in this country to sign up with at least one of them.

Questions for Readers

1. What evidence do you have that the connections between all educational stakeholders in your area are improving?

2. How might you increase the impact of professional networks in your area?

3. How does your country encourage collaboration between schools?

Chapter 6
The Future Is Happening Now—Assessment

Would you believe me if I said that, in New Zealand school assessment, there are few correct answers? Sounds crazy, doesn't it? Let me reassure you: there are still wrong or weak answers. But we focus on something other than just reconfirming known facts about the world when we assess the potential of young people.

SOLO Taxonomy

Our national grading system is based on a combination of Bloom's[1] and SOLO[2] taxonomy. As an educator, you probably know Bloom's, but it's less likely, especially in America, that you've heard of SOLO (Structure of Observed Learning Outcomes). This system looks at

---

1 "Bloom's taxonomy - Wikipedia, the free encyclopedia." 2011. 11 May 2016, https://en.wikipedia.org/wiki/Bloom's_taxonomy
2 "Structure of observed learning outcome - Wikipedia, the free ..." 2015. 11 May 2016, https://en.wikipedia.org/wiki/Structure_of_observed_learning_outcome

the depth of genuine understanding and was first proposed by the Australian educational psychologist, John B. Biggs in 1982. The model consists of five levels of understanding:

1. **Pre-structural**—The task is not attacked appropriately; the student hasn't really understood the point and uses too simple a way of going about it.
2. **Uni-structural**—The student's response only focuses on one relevant aspect.
3. **Multi-structural**—The student's response focuses on several relevant aspects, but they are treated independently and additively. Assessment of this level is primarily quantitative.
4. **Relational**—The different aspects have become integrated into a coherent whole. This level is what is typically described as an adequate understanding of a topic.
5. **Extended Abstract**—The previous integrated whole may be conceptualised at a higher level of abstraction and generalised to a new topic or area.[3]

In the graphic on the next page you'll see how I use both for professional development with teachers and with the students to teach them how they will be graded in all subjects. For high school graduation, every assessment of knowledge and competency is graded as "Not Achieved" (Pre-structural), "Achieved" (Uni-/Multi-structural), "Merit" (Relational), and "Excellence" (Extended abstract).

---

3   "SOLO Taxonomy | John Biggs." 2013. 11 May 2016,
    http://www.johnbiggs.com.au/academic/solo-taxonomy/

  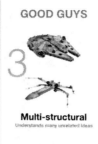 

Pre-structural	Uni-structural	Multi-structural	Relational
Incomplete understanding	Understands an idea	Understands many unrelated ideas	Explains the relationship between the separate ideas

THE
HAN
SOLO
TAXONOMY
By @EduWells
EduWells.com

WHAT WOULD RON WESLEY DO?

Extended abstract
Can explain the significance of these relationships within the wider context. Move learning in to a new context. You have to really know both Star Wars and Harry Potter to explain what Ron might do in a Star Wars scene.

Imagine watching *Star Wars IV: A New Hope* with your class. You know, that's the first *Star Wars* film—the one that released in 1977 and was made primarily with yoghurt containers. The following day you ask students about the film and divide the answers into five Solo groups:

1. The "Pre-structural" students can say it was a film about blowing up the space station.

2. The "Uni-structural" students can name the Death Star and say it was a space station for the baddy Empire.

3. The "Multi-structural" students can name the Death Star and also the X-wings as goody fighter planes. They name a number of characters, too.

4. The "Relational" Students can group the characters together as goodies and baddies and explain what they are fighting about, i.e., the relationships to indicate the narrative. This is what you would normally describe as understanding the film enough to explain its story; doing so effectively requires an understanding of the relationships between elements.

5. The "Extended Abstract" students have such an understanding of narrative and character relationships they can contextualise them against other stories or films. For example, here's a question: Would Ron be friends with Luke? To explain how Ron Weasley from Harry Potter would relate to Luke Skywalker, you not only have to know Luke's story but also his priorities in life and how Ron would respond to these. Being able to compare and contrast within external contexts is to show full understanding of a topic or issue.

(How courses are developed to cater best for this grading system is covered in the next chapter.)

Whether a school is still utilising standardised exams, designing their own project assessments, or even negotiating assessments with students, the work and answers will be judged using the approach inspired by SOLO taxonomy. In this country, even the traditional standardised exam questions take an approach based on SOLO. Rather than look at a total number of correct answers, all questions are categorised (although this is not published to the student) as one of four thinking levels. We only have four because we have combined SOLO's uni-structural and multi-structural levels to form a single "pass" level, or as we call it, "achieved." The final grade is determined by the type of questions in which the student succeeded, which reveals their level of ability in the particular topic/standard on which the exam is focused. This might mean that a talented student doesn't waste time with short or easy questions and makes better use of exam time by focusing on more challenging ones.

If you want more information, then connect with Pam Hook (@ arti_choke). She's the best author and speaker on the topic. She's also hilarious, and I highly recommend catching her at a conference if you can.

NCEA—Standard-Based Assessment That Works

The National Certificate in Educational Achievement (NCEA) is a standards-based assessment, generally untaken by school students aged fourteen to sixteen. In Year 11 (K10), students work towards NCEA Level 1, which they achieve if they succeed at standards that collectively offer eighty credits. Level 2 is mostly attempted by seventeen-year-olds, who achieve it by succeeding at standards that offer sixty Level 2 credits. Level 3 credit standards are generally attempted by eighteen-year-olds in Year 13 (K12). So far, this assessment may sound typical of any number of school systems around the world. So what's the difference?

It is true that many schools in New Zealand are still working through changes to their approach to learning and thus are still running standardised exams that expect predetermined answers. What I'm going to explain here is that the New Zealand education system and its assessment are flexible enough to allow any public school to move away from standardised testing completely, *whilst still offering the same nationally recognised high school qualification*. If a school leadership team and/or teachers come to see the learning pitfalls in standardised testing, New Zealand's assessment system is prepared for them to design a whole new approach they feel is more appropriate for their students.

The library of NCEA Standards consists of thousands of purposefully open-ended competency and knowledge topic standards. The examples listed show the variety of topics:

For seventeen- to eighteen-year-olds...

- "Demonstrate understanding of oxidation-reduction."
- "Develop an informed understanding of literature and/or language using critical texts."
- "Apply linear programming methods in solving problems."
- "Analyse different perspectives of a contested event of significance to New Zealanders."

For fifteen- to sixteen-year-olds...

- "Demonstrate understanding of life processes at the cellular level."
- "Explain the operation of the traditional Māori economy."
- "Demonstrate geographic understanding of an urban pattern."
- "Take action to enhance an aspect of people's well-being within the school or wider community."

Each of these *standards* is outlined on a three- or four-page document explaining the evidence that NCEA assessors would be expecting to see at all three achievement levels: achieved, merit, and excellence. The open-ended design of these standards is meant to allow teachers and, more recently, students to devise projects and work that would best show excellence-level thinking and understanding.

The other primary purpose of the standards-based approach is that teachers and students can develop projects using collections of standards from different disciplines. This way, an authentic project with the power to make real change in a community could be devised. For example, a project's demand for communication, scientific experiment, product design, marketing, and evaluation could all be assessed by the relevant standards and possibly offer a student around half his or her qualification needs for the year.

As explained in the official NCEA introductory video,[4] the primary reason for shifting away from standardised, high-stakes testing and towards skills and knowledge standards is to reflect a learner's whole educational experience. It allows us to credit students equally for all of their talents, be they creative, practical, or academic.

Now what if students could design their own high school graduation assessment? That sounds even crazier than having very few "correct answers," doesn't it? Maybe, but the schools that have utilised NCEA's

---

4   "How NCEA works video » NZQA." 2014. 11 May 2016,
    http://www.nzqa.govt.nz/qualifications-standards/qualifications/
    ncea/understanding-ncea/how-ncea-works/video/

flexibility the most have been exploring the possibility and feasibility of student-negotiated qualification projects. This kind of shift doesn't happen overnight. But the students who will be the first to design their own graduation assessments will have been through a public schooling that required this approach to learning and thus are prepared to plan and run projects for their high school graduation. They will have to work with their teachers to understand available topic standards and how each of the standards is graded. This means that each student has to work with a number of specialist teachers, who each know different details about their specialty's standards in order to piece together how their project will provide evidence and gain all the available credits.

Now let's take it a step further. I can tell you that under NCEA, for some standards, students are allowed to submit a group's output and each receive the grade awarded for it. This might be common in many schools around the world, but probably not for high school graduation and qualifications. In New Zealand, however, students are expected to record their contributions, and teachers are entrusted to award an appropriate grade. This is useful, in particular, for learning areas such as dance, where individuals add different but equally important elements to a filmed performance. The video can be stored for moderating the awarded grades with other educators.

Although it seems wonderful to me that New Zealand has successfully instigated such things as group grading, student-designed assessment, and cross-curricular graduation, it hasn't been a straightforward journey. Let me show you just how messy a business it is to transform the approach towards assessment—and change the mindset of an entire nation.

The Uncomfortable Shift towards Personalised High School Assessment

As I provide a more detailed look into the introduction of New Zealand's high school assessment, you'll notice that it wasn't an easy road to travel. While I believe the rewards—for students and teachers, both at high school and in lower grades—are worth the effort, make no mistake: the shift required massive effort and commitment. If your school (or country) is just beginning the process, I hope you'll take comfort in slow progress. Know that it may take a decade before you see significant progress. But in those interim years, I believe you will see the steady transformation of mindset held by high school teachers, and imagine the relief felt by elementary and middle school teachers who no longer have to be so constrained in the way they prepare younger students for future schooling. Remember, NCEA is our assessment system used for the final three years of high school.

The First Five Years: "Surely, they're just new tests."

When NCEA was introduced, it was replacing a traditional examination system. The generation of teachers in place to promote a standards-based assessment were capable—but not experienced or prepared—enough to make the most of it. As you might expect, there were numerous logistical problems involved in ensuring all teachers were aware of how the new assessment system worked and what it would mean to their teaching.

Unfortunately, not enough buildup, training, or information had passed on from the educators and ministry who had devised it to the rest of the educators who were to deliver it. For the first five years, most standards were assessed in standardised tests, retaining the format the teachers knew best and completely missing the point for making the shift to NCEA. Standardised exams, in particular, were not a format that could make the most of assessing understanding levels over raw facts.

Another issue when switching to a new style of assessment was public awareness and opinion. The schools themselves were still grappling with fully understanding the potential of NCEA after five years, so you can imagine the confusion amongst the public. Newspapers were quick to pick fault with the new system and sell copy highlighting the various mistakes that were being made across the country. Being a teacher-driven, high-trust model, there were also initial problems with moderating teachers' grade judgements. A tiny number of teachers were also discovered issuing credits inappropriately for little actual work. I would credit the relaxed Kiwi approach to life to the fact that these minor hiccups didn't lead to any drastic kneejerk political interference. Thankfully, NCEA remained intact and was left to develop and improve.

NCEA's designers understood from the beginning that the shift would require time. They were playing a "long game" for what is now an excellent system.

The Second Five Years: "Oh. Teachers can design projects?"

During the first five messy years, teachers continually received training, information, and peer support. By the time I arrived in the country from the United Kingdom in 2006, some teachers and schools were adopting the more flexible approach and allowing for student choice within the assessments they were designing. Teachers began to design projects that encapsulated two or more standards in larger pieces of work. Learning areas such as technology were able to switch from assessing isolated skill competencies (such as making a webpage or robot) to large, product-development projects issuing credits for developing briefs and analysing markets and stakeholders for their technology products.

As an example of teachers allowing students to personalise their assessments, one teacher whose school was alongside the beach created a sustainability project based around surfboard product development, where students had to build fully recyclable boards that catered to specific surfers' performance needs as well as their rather fussy design preferences. This project utilised five NCEA Standards, earning students a quarter of their year's requirements in credits.

Although this might sound like great stuff, the truth is that in 2015, most New Zealand high schools still feel challenged by the idea of shifting completely away from isolated subject specialisation. Some schools have broken the conventional mould completely, and an increasing number of schools now offer students an open choice in how they want to be assessed, what teacher-designed projects they want to attempt, and, most importantly, only about 20 percent of final graduation assessment is done through standardised examination.

The Third Five Years: "Wow! Student-designed assessment!"

Now this is where the story gets really exciting for me. A combination of strong experience in standard-based assessment, new pedagogies, and teacher growth mindset are all coming together in some New Zealand schools to build what I think is the most secure and future-focused education in the world. Like I mentioned before, by focusing on the conditions for high school graduation qualifications in this way, the entire school system now develops and prepares learners to be capable of designing and managing their own educational achievement.

The entire school system now develops and prepares learners to be capable of designing and managing their own educational achievement.

New Zealand has begun to reverse the normal approach. In most educational systems, the qualification determines the student focus and output, especially standardised exams. Here, students are now starting to negotiate how their projects at school will attain the national high school qualifications. In some cases this might be one of the following:

- a small project to sign off on just one topic standard (e.g., "graphing")
- a subject-based project to achieve a number of standards (e.g., a multifaceted science project)
- a larger cross-curricular project achieving numerous standards and possibly making up a major slice of a student's annual qualifications

I have personally seen the power individual ownership over the whole process has in engaging students in learning. As we move deeper into this current phase, the concept of cross-curricular projects (something that seemed like a pipe dream at the start of NCEA) is becoming a reality. Initially, teachers only saw themselves as possible designers/ authors of such projects, and the complicated nature of these projects created a potentially daunting workload. Now that schools are preparing students to design accountable projects, the entire system seems more plausible. The focus now is to ensure the students' assessment projects meet a national standard so as to maintain a credible qualification system.

Moderation

So the big question you may be asking is, "How is all this held together across the country with schools, teachers, and students all personalising assessment to meet their needs?" Well, again, it rests on the level of trust the government has in the teachers to maintain high standards by collaborating and sharing practice as part of the system.

Every aspect of the process is moderated at three stages:

1. Assessment plan and material check (before use)
2. Internal teacher's grade moderation (after use)
3. National moderation of teacher grades (samples and grades sent to national moderators)

Assessment Plan and Material Check (before Use)

When a teacher and/or student designs a project and its respective assessment matrix to match the requirements of one or more standards, the plan, guidance material, and marking matrix all have to be signed off on by another educator. This might be colleagues within the school or teachers from another school. Connecting with other schools for moderation is generally understood as best practice. This evaluation must be done before the project gets underway and must include judgement statements or examples of potential evidence within the work that would achieve each of the three NCEA grades: achieved, merit, and excellence.

In schools that implement the graduation-assessment approach, high school subject specialists within the school are consulted to ensure the elements will meet each subject standard's requirements.

Internal Teacher's Grade Moderation (after Use)

Two English teachers in a school might teach the same standard but with a focus on different novels. Two technology teachers might both assess students on prototyping but with different materials such as textiles or engineering with metal. The NCEA system asks that teachers exchange samples of their marking and agree that they are making the same judgements regarding the thinking and understanding levels on display in the student work. This is signed off on official internal moderation documentation. The quality of this process in each school is checked by visits from the government's Education Review Office (ERO).

National Moderation of Teacher Grades

Once a year, the New Zealand Qualification Authority (NZQA), who manages NCEA assessments, requests a random sample of thirty to forty standards that have been used by a school. The grading of each standard is checked by a large team of national moderators (NZQA-trained educators paid extra for the duty) who receive a sample of eight student works. They write a report as to how much the grade decisions align with national guidelines. Over the years, New Zealand has done a brilliant job of developing a good understanding of how to grade each standard, and the number of discrepancies has diminished each year. There have been complaints and bad press regarding the tiny number of incorrect gradings, but it's a minor issue that is being sorted amongst a huge number of obvious benefits—many of which I hope this book is highlighting.

Supporting Teachers to Lead Education and Assessment

When your curriculum is clear of content, and your education system is designed by the educators themselves (who are busy in their classrooms), I would forgive you for wondering who has the time to coordinate it all. Over the past decade, a number of support systems and resources have been developed from which teachers can seek guidance and training. The overall approach for all stages of schooling is one that expects New Zealand educators to be connected and sharing good practices through these systems and national online communities. The following organisations provide essential support systems and connect teachers and schools to the resources and training they need to succeed.

NZQA—New Zealand Qualifications Authority

NZQA is a government organisation working under the ministry for education. It is responsible for funding and supporting teachers to build the assessment system. Its site[5] contains the high school assessment standards, teaching resources as well as exemplars of previously submitted student work. Again, I must stress that, like the curriculum, this site and the NCEA system serve only as a framework upon which the teachers should base their assessments. The style, focus, and approach are still in the hands of individual teachers, whilst they ensure their students meet the standards and gain the accreditation on offer.

Standards are always under review and, every year, many will have minor improvements made to them based on teacher recommendations. NZQA is also in charge of the moderation process that takes place between teachers and schools. The organisation expects a randomly selected sample of evidence from each school to be submitted by sets of student URLs, which point to blogs, cloud documents, videos, or full websites. These are the output from students who have attempted to meet the standards. NZQA provides funding for teachers to become national moderators and produces annual reports to highlight assessment issues that should be examined by schools so as to align understandings and expectations for the assessments.

TKI—Te Kete Ipurangi (The Internet Basket)

All this teacher-led assessment is supported by a number of resources and government-funded organisations. These provide guidance, discussion, and training to ensure teachers are delivering best practices. The primary teacher support site is tki.org.nz,[6] which includes frameworks, documentation, moderation links, and training opportunities. It also includes guidance and connections for school leaders on helping them lead twenty-first-century schools. A fantastic example of the type of support this site offers is its separate site dedicated to

---

5 "NCEA - NZQA." 2010. 10 Apr. 2016,
　　http://www.nzqa.govt.nz/qualifications-standards/qualifications/ncea/
6 "Homepage - Te Kete Ipurangi (TKI)." 2006. 9 Apr. 2016, https://www.tki.org.nz

inclusive education, inclusive.tki.org.nz.[7] This resource offers inspiring examples and guidance on supporting all learners, regardless of their personal challenges, to achieve and enjoy the process of learning. TKI grows every year and is largely built by educators with numerous resources for twenty-first-century learning such as universal design for learning or project-based learning.

Team Solutions—Auckland University Faculty of Education

Auckland University[8] trains many new teachers for New Zealand. It also offers professional development within schools for existing teachers. This is effectively a free service provided by government funding, and the training consists of anything from one-day training to long-term projects. Teachers can also request information on virtually any aspect of teaching from pedagogy to assessment. Team Solutions, the professional development arm of the university's education faculty, is staffed by educators, many of whom are employed for short periods (two or three years) to run professional development projects or research, after which they return to teaching posts in schools. This keeps the advice offered grounded in current practice and challenges. One Team Solutions staff member recently highlighted the reciprocal benefits of being able to alternate between teaching and research at Auckland University. As a New Zealand educator, she could spend three years researching and training with Team Solutions to keep her teaching practice relevant, followed by a few years teaching to keep her research grounded in reality. Other New Zealand universities offer similar services to other parts of the country.

---

7   "Inclusive Education - Guides for schools - TKI." 2014. 9 Apr. 2016,
    http://inclusive.tki.org.nz/
8   "Team Solutions - The University of Auckland." 2014. 10 Apr. 2016,
    http://www.education.auckland.ac.nz/en/about/professional-development/
    team-solutions-home.html

A Self-Supporting Education Ecosystem

The deep involvement of educators in creating the assessment system has led to a sense that it is fluid and always improving itself. Regardless of the age of students being taught, the teachers themselves feel an obligation to improve the school experience each year. They are empowered and thus motivated by the freedom and respect the government shows them to develop the best system possible. The above agencies, plus many others, provide support and guidance (rather than acting as education overlords) like many countries' administrations. Instead of a typical top-down approach, it is far more exciting and positive to be working in a collaborative, "bottom-up" education community. I believe and hope the processes and connections that shape the education sector in New Zealand are embedded enough that it doesn't backtrack. I have seen evidence that both sides of our political system are supportive, so—fingers crossed—we'll be OK.

Questions for Readers

1. How does the administration of your country's education support or restrict educators to adapt learning to suit the times in which we live?

2. How collaborative is the development of education between schools and government?

3. What might be your first steps in starting a fifteen-year process to personalised assessment?

Chapter 7
Our Best Examples
Can Be Found Anywhere

Amazing innovation can occur in a system in which teachers are encouraged to challenge the structures of the status quo and devise solutions to best suit the needs of learners. Pair that philosophy with trust, clear goals, and an inquiry model that promotes constant growth, and *everything* about the way learning takes place changes.

In previous chapters, I've explained the numerous seeds that were sewn in an effort to grow New Zealand's flexible, future-focused education system. The results of all that planting and cultivating can be seen in the innovative examples I will share in this chapter.

I'll give you fair warning: In the next few pages, you'll read about schools that may or may not have lessons, classrooms, subjects, teachers, and even ... wait for it ... *tests*. Remember that New Zealand schools are autonomous in the way they approach learning. This means we have public schools, both traditional and futuristic. However, those pushing the envelope are getting many people in this country and around the world very excited, hence, this book. I've included examples from each age group in the hopes that all teachers can learn something from these exemplary schools. I hope you'll see how the approaches taken by these schools lead to almost seamless education for the learners as they progress from one school to the next.

Early Childhood

Kids' Domain
Kidsdomain.co.nz

I visited this early childhood learning centre in 2015 as part of a research project I carried out with CORE Education (NZ). Here, I saw two- to four-year-olds being educated in a terrifically challenging and respectful way. The student involvement in the design of their education was particularly impressive. You could see the impact of this respectful approach in the confidence the senior four-year-olds showed when discussing the programmes and learning taking place. Kids' Domain is a fantastic example of educators analysing and implementing the New Zealand Curriculum in all aspects of their operation. Here's how the school explains its approach:

> *Children are placed at the centre of curriculum negotiations, the belief being that they learn best when their interests are acknowledged as worthy of investigation. Once an area of interest is identified, children are encouraged to become involved in an inquiry approach to learning that stimulates the generation of questions, thoughtful investigation, and playful exploration of ideas.*[1]

Not many kindergartens have a design-thinking space for such things as rethinking public amenities. At Kids' Domain, they do. Students were taken on a field trip to a multi-storey car park (parking garage) to look at how cars navigated and parked within the space. Teachers videoed what students saw. When the students returned to school, they set about building and discussing new parking buildings

---

1 "Environments for Living and Learning - Kids' Domain." 2011. 11 May 2016, http://www.kidsdomain.co.nz/environments-for-living-and-learning

whilst the video played on a loop on one of the walls. Although building connects children with the elements of design and the working of the system, in reality, what the children produced may or may not necessarily work as a public parking area. That's not what's important here. What *is* important is the level of thinking and aspiration the school promotes. The development of new knowledge and self-esteem that comes from feeling as if you might have a say in how the world operates is paramount if you are to encourage lifelong learning. Educators at Kid's Domain take their students' views seriously, whilst ensuring fun and excitement is maintained.

The design of every learning space at Kids' Domain opens to outdoors. The open and flexible indoor areas contain different types of spaces, including climbing zones. Students are free to explore and reinvent the spaces as they see fit.

This is the school I mentioned in Chapter 5 that has a leadership programme for the senior four-year-olds. These young students discuss what leadership should look and sound like. They are also consulted on a number of decisions regarding the design of their learning programme at the school.

One aspect of professional expectation, as encouraged by the national curriculum framework that Kids' Domain exemplifies, is that of ongoing research. The school explains on its website why the research project, "Lived Childhood Experiences: A Collective Storytelling Approach to Professional Learning for Innovation and Equality," is important:

> *In 2009, Kids' Domain began an action research project on collective storytelling. Over three years, teachers shared and disrupted storylines of childhood, teaching and life experiences, troubling diversity, difference, and identity. The project has contributed to teachers' understandings and practice of teaching for innovation and equity.[2]*

2   "Teaching Teams - Kids' Domain." 2011. 11 May 2016, http://www.kidsdomain.co.nz/teaching-teams

I know this kind of commitment and research is not unique, but it is rare to find early childhood centres involving all staff in action research.[3] It serves as an impressive example of how New Zealand's educational culture promotes continual inquiry by teachers. In fact, it seems natural to reflect and study one's results when working in an education system that asks the teachers to choose content and approach. If you, the teacher, have made such key choices for what others will be doing, you will be inclined to check the success of those decisions.

Elementary/Primary

Taupaki Primary School,
Principal Stephen Lethbridge
taupaki.school.nz

When it comes to world-leading elementary and middle schooling, Taupaki Primary School near Auckland has everything in place. Future-focused board members, who care so much that they blog on education, a principal who performs TEDx Talks on education reform, educators who use design thinking and makerspaces to challenge students to form new knowledge, and all this in a school system that demands a personalised approach to learning.

Stephen Lethbridge is an educator and principal who enjoys challenging schools to take a full and reflective look at whether the service they provide is meeting the needs of learners in the twenty-first century. His school is on the other side of Auckland from mine, but I know a number of teachers at Taupaki Primary School, all of whom are doing fantastic and inspiring work.

Like me, Stephen is determined to develop independent learners who naturally collaborate to build new knowledge. He explains that personal responsibility in learning is an integral part of education:

---

3   Action research is either research initiated to solve an immediate problem or a reflective process of progressive problem solving led by individuals working with others in teams or as part of a "community of practice" to improve the way they address issues and solve problems. - Wikipedia

*We are starting to see classes from years four–eight use indi-
vidual learning plans where children plan their week based upon
their data; they opt into teaching clinics, and in some cases run
teaching clinics for others. This is a natural extension in our AfL
[Assessment for Learning] journey. We are starting to see the
practical implementation of personalised learning unfold.*[4]

There are some questions I would rather not hear students ask, such
as, "What are we doing today?" Likewise, Stephen aims for his school
to develop *"self-motivated learners, children who develop a capacity to
know what to do when they don't know what to do."*[5] Taupaki Primary
School is another example of success in a student-driven learning environment. Too many educators around the world are fearful of creating
a student-led education model. But Stephen has put in place school
structures and a collaborative network of teachers, parents, and board
members who are passionate about building (and modelling) self-reg-
ulated learning.

Here are just two examples of how different Taupaki's approach is
from many elementary schools:

1. **Students actively use their own data.** Stephen says, "We
    encourage students to look at their assessment data and
    make choices about what teaching clinics they need in order
    to progress their learning." In most schools, assessment data
    is something that is seen as a communication tool between
    teacher and student or, worse, only between the teacher and
    parent. It is normally used as an indication of whether a stu-
    dent needs to work harder or deserves a pat on the back. At
    Taupaki, the school promotes assessment for learning (AfL).
    Data is not exclusively for teachers' use. Students use it as well
    to shape their own future learning. AfL works because the

---

4   "Enabling Responsibility | Leading Today." 2014. 13 Feb. 2016,
    http://stephenlethbridge.com/?p=218
5   "The Road to Self-Regulation | Leading Today." 2014. 13 Feb. 2016,
    http://stephenlethbridge.com/?p=228

students are not all having education delivered to them and are free to navigate their own path. And remember, these children are younger than ten! As Stephen puts it, "Our approach is grounded in valid and reliable 'hard' data. Yet the way we use the data develops the broader goal of self-regulation."

2. **Active governance supports personalisation**: "The Board of Trustees have also adopted a Governance as Inquiry approach in order to stay true to the intent of our vision,"[6] Stephen explains. The current Board Chair for Taupaki Primary School, Paula Hogg (@diana_prince_ww), explains on her blog why inquiry is important at all levels:

> We wanted to improve and deepen our curriculum reviews and self-review. What we didn't want was a tick-box compliance method where standard industry questions were asked and existing evidence was found to show compliance. This type of review typically does not result in deep changes in practice; it often results in minor tweaks and more of the status quo.[7]

Like Kids' Domain, Taupaki Primary School promotes teachers as learners and highly values the responsibility to model good learning behaviours. Stephen notes the following:

> As leaders in schools (and I mean leaders in the broadest possible sense), it is our responsibility to model these behaviours to our children. It is our responsibility to think aloud, to share our thought processes so that our children know that learning is a challenge, we never stop doing it, and that we can always get better with practice and support from the collective group.[8]

---

6 "Staying true to the Vision | Leading Today." 2014. 13 Feb. 2016, http://stephenlethbridge.com/?p=240
7 "Governance as Inquiry: Episode I – Confessions from the chair." 2014. 13 Feb. 2016, http://paula.h4.co.nz/?p=212
8 "Modelling a Growth Mindset | Leading Today." 2015. 27 Feb. 2016, http://stephenlethbridge.com/?p=305

The challenge for New Zealand middle and high schools is to be prepared to receive learners who are accustomed to the sort of empowered status that elementary schools like Taupaki Primary School develop. Fortunately, we have many excellent middle and high schools. In the next section, I'll introduce you to a public middle school that continues to demonstrate excellence in education.

Middle / Intermediate School

Breens Intermediate School, Principal Brian Price

When Christchurch, the largest city on the south island of New Zealand, experienced a powerful and extremely destructive earthquake in 2011, the hard-hit city centre was left with mountains of rubble where buildings once stood. Away from the city centre, most buildings, including a school called Breens Intermediate, suffered damage.[9] This sixth and seventh grade school had always operated quite conventionally, with students assigned to a home classroom and a teacher. The earthquake damaged rooms and thus forced a rethink. The principal at the time, Brian Price (@BrianPrice007), had been considering new pedagogy, especially in regards to better reflecting the bi-cultural aspect of New Zealand education. Brian realised that this moment of tragedy provided the opportunity to enact significant change in the school's approach to education.

9   "Breens Intermediate: Welcome." 2013. 14 Mar. 2016,
    http://breens.ultranet.school.nz

An Alternative to Conventional Schooling with Positive Outcomes

I visited the school in 2015 and was completely impressed by what Brian and Breens Intermediate School had achieved. They had repurposed their existing physical classroom and corridor spaces and had redesigned their timetable to create a whole new learning experience. I could see within ten minutes that the students were more driven and positive about school than in most schools visited.

The school managed this transition by dividing itself into mini-schools within the site. Rather than each student being confined to a particular room from which learning would be *received*, students now have permission to design their own school days (every day). They have free access to up to four differently purposed rooms that they can choose based on what their needs are at any particular moment, plus shared areas, inside and outside.

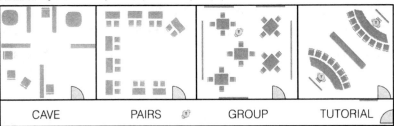

21st CENTURY SCHOOL IN 20th CENTURY BUILDINGS

By Richard Wells ⓒ EduWells
more at EduWells.com

The conventional schooling approach where a student is only permitted one room for an allotted time does not develop genuine skills in independence and resilience. The more practice young people get at independently organising their day, their learning and the help they need, the more they will perfect these skills desperately needed in a rapidly changing world. In this model, most learning is done through negotiated inquiry projects, either as individuals or groups. The whole school day is controlled by the student and they use any of the four allocated rooms and book into tutorials as they need. The same four teachers cover the overall space they used to. They teach tutorials on a rotation and mentor students in the other 3 rooms at all other times. Evidence from schools that have used this shows students becoming more confident and driven by the ownership they have over their learning and the space provided.

| CAVE | PAIRS | GROUP | TUTORIAL |

The Cave is the silent room for study, reading and reflecting. No noise allowed! Dividers, bookshelves, beanbags and comfortable chairs help students relax and isolate themselves when needed.

A pairs room is for quiet discussion and peer tutoring. The desk configuration encourages the students to stick to the quiet pair work rule.

The group room is noisier and allows teams to hold project meetings or plan inquiries into new learning. Whiteboards around the walls help team planning and brainstorming

Students book into one of two tutorials in specialised subject areas or general Q & A sessions each half-hour. Only 10 spots available per tutorial. The room includes central seating that allows for silent observation of tutorial for those wanting repeats or not needing to Question.

= TEACHER

Idea based on system at Breens Intermediate School (New Zealand)

New Use of School Space

Children have free access to four different kinds of rooms:
- Caves (silent study / reflection rooms)
- Pairs (rooms for peer tutoring)
- Groups (rooms set up for projects / teamwork)
- Tutorial (rooms students can book for teacher-guided tutorials)

These will seem familiar to anyone who has read the work by David D. Thornburg on caves, mountains, campfires, and watering holes,[10] but remember, these were middle school students using any of these spaces at any point during any day. It was up to the children to use these spaces according to needs and to be responsible for productive time management.

It was very evident during my visit that, as the result of practice and extensive experience in self-driven learning, the average student was confident, organised, and keen to discuss his or her progress. Multiple students approached me and the other visitors to instigate conversations and showcase their work. Rather than prepared presentations or specific instructions from their teachers about what to do, say, or share, students were trusted to do their work. In fact, the principal made a point of refusing to accompany us through the school; he knew the children would welcome us themselves with pride to showcase the school they ran themselves.

---

10 Thornburg, DD. "Campfires in Cyberspace," The Thornburg Center for Professional Development. 2012. http://tcpd.org/Thornburg/Handouts/Campfires.pdf

New Use of School Time

At Breens Intermediate School, students are free to organise their own day. They must schedule a certain amount of tutoring in a week, but even with that requirement, they are able to tailor the tutoring to their needs. Students negotiate inquiry projects at the beginning of terms and work on them in teams. They are encouraged to work together and solve their own problems. Rather than assuming technology is a must all day, the school allows students to check out technology from a central hub on an as-needed basis.

When I have talked with teachers from other schools, even some in New Zealand, their most common question is, "How do students cope with this responsibility?" For this, I have two answers:

1. After their first two weeks, most students adapt to what is simply the new norm. It's amazing what children are capable of if expectations are raised. It's frightening to think about the potential that is lost when teachers cling to lower expectations of students and feel the need to shape every moment of the day.

2. Student-driven environments create more time for teachers to support those who need it. The teachers I spoke to at Breens said they felt more relaxed than when they operated in the traditional school model. They told me that the new approach allows them to offer more support to students. It wasn't surprising to hear them say they would never return to conventional schooling.

New Use of Teachers

Teachers rotate between giving tutorials and roaming as mentors. The principal signs off on the final projects (a nice touch). Teachers have more time to talk to students and guide teams in their negotiated inquiries. Teachers enjoy working with students who are intrinsically motivated to learn on projects designed in part or wholly by themselves. They use evidence of learning based on those projects to report on students' progress towards national standards—progress they are able to witness during each day of mentoring. All the national curriculum and regular content still gets covered, and direct teaching is still available to students when it's needed. But learning at Breens is never delivered in a one-size-fits-all approach. All in all, the workload for the educators is not less, just different. Teachers spend more time discussing and recording progress and less time designing lessons for all students to receive every day.

As I walked around the school during that visit, the busy atmosphere and smiling teachers offered proof that this new system worked for Breens. My colleagues and I left the school immensely impressed with what we had seen. The experience felt genuine. This wasn't a show that had been put on; it was a learning environment that motivated students through empowerment. What I had seen that day led me to ask the obvious question: Why are most other schools *not* like this?

The educators with me on the visit were all equally impressed, which made me think a familiar flaw in education must have been at play, namely a lack of communication and relationships between schools. It isn't a common practice for schools to promote their practices to the world and thus, even in New Zealand, the brilliance of Breens Intermediate School was hidden from view. When I blogged about this school's educational success, I was not at all surprised by the thousands of Retweets and positive responses their story received.[11] Here's the lesson: Be willing to try a new approach. And whether it works or fails, be willing to share your experience and results.

---

11 https://eduwells.com/2015/11/21/hey-teacher-would-you-be-a-student/

Design a School *You* Would Want to Attend

If you ask me, the elephant in the classroom, especially in high school classrooms, has always been the fact that teachers would rarely choose for themselves the daily experience they inflict on their students. This truth is particularly evident when teachers are discussing professional development days, where suggestions of separate, unrelated sessions throughout the day and a bombardment of information not tailored to the individual needs of each teacher are met with anger and resentment. The last thing teachers want is anything that resembles a day at school.

If you ask high school teachers if they'd be happy with a daily experience that included...

- an hour of trigonometry;
- an hour of Macbeth;
- an hour of plate tectonics;
- an hour of tennis, followed by
- an hour of chemical reactions;
- no attempt to relate any of the learning,
- and closing it out with an hour-long assembly with teenagers,

nearly all teachers would say NO! (I've asked many.)

 # Two Questions for Teachers

1. What excuses do we have for creating a learning experience we wouldn't choose for ourselves?

2. Why are we surprised at an increasing dropout rate and general switching off from school in a connected and active world of Facebook and YouTube?

High Schools

Hobsonville Point School,
Principal Maurie Abraham
hpss.school.nz

"It's the school's responsibility to lead the community in education and not be led by them," says Maurie Abraham, principal of Hobsonville Point Secondary School. Hobsonville is a newly developed area in Auckland, and this includes new schools and amenities. The fact that these public schools are new is sometimes mistakenly given as the reason why they can take such "crazy" approaches to education. I say "mistakenly" because, after visiting many schools like Hobsonville Point School, I know it is not the physical space or the newness that creates the difference; it's the people and mindsets held by those who designed the approach to learning.

When the elementary and high school buildings were constructed in Hobsonville, both were built with the same open-plan designs. What the leaders have produced in these public schools is impressive enough that they have had visitors from schools across New Zealand as well as Australia, Singapore, Korea, and the United States.

During the process of founding the schools, the leadership team decided to analyse every aspect of learning and to make the most of New Zealand's flexible curriculum. They scrutinised the curriculum, breaking down each of its values and expectations. Then they added in the best future-focused practices from around the world, carefully scouring research and examples to visualise and design how their schools would operate. The desire was to best achieve the aims of the curriculum document and cater to the needs of twenty-first-century learners. This process led to a whole new approach to formal schooling.

I am good friends with a number of the teachers at these schools and, after visiting several times and meeting with the principal, teachers, and students, I picked up on four themes that drive the schools' daily operation. These are not the schools' official four aims, rather they are the impressions and feelings one gets from the teachers and students when you're there as a visitor:

1. Future ready
2. Student driven
3. Bias towards authentic impact on the world
4. As little standardisation as possible

In the high school, every time slot on the timetable is dedicated to student-driven and designed projects and reflection. For the projects, issues and topics are brought up for consideration by students and teachers. From those topics, students plan, either in groups or independently, how to best tackle the projects and how to ensure the learning process leads to real outcomes. The result of these projects is that the school is having quite an impact on the local community. The school also dedicates specific time for students and teachers to reflect on their learning. These reflection sessions take up considerable time on the timetable, showing a true dedication to this important aspect of learning. An indication of the success of this reflection time is that many Hobsonville students blog about learning and education by choice.

I've met Principal Maurie Abraham on a number of occasions. I have also worked quite a bit with the teachers from his school. Maurie and his school exemplify world-leading education. The school may consist of open-plan, modern learning environments, but I must be clear that it is Maurie's leadership that compels me to write about his school. The central reason for his successful leadership of future-focused education is that he and his school endeavour to link every decision to their vision for education. His school makes the most of the autonomy New Zealand offers schools by breaking almost every rule of conventional, twentieth-century, factory-style education. When he explains his vision and practice, it is evident that his primary concern is serving the needs of his learners in relation to current research and world events—and the future towards which they are heading. His is an approach that contrasts sharply with conventional academia, which, from my experience as both student and educator, often remains separated from what's going on around it.

Like the leaders at the other schools I've mentioned in this chapter, Maurie expects everyone in his school—teachers, students, and support staff—to be active learners who challenge assumptions and constantly ask those *unGoogleable* questions. He and the community of educators he leads are on a mission to encourage the rest of New Zealand's schools to create more of the fantastic opportunities I've outlined in this book. Maurie explains, "We are doing this because we are committed to bringing life to the potential of the NZC and to make secondary schooling more relevant for young people."[12]

The school uses a "relationship-based pedagogy," which itself has impacts on the decisions and ways in which the school functions. Traditional, teacher-centric classrooms don't generate the sort of learning relationships for which Hobsonville aims. That's why the school has longer learning periods than most schools, with significant time allocated to learner reflection. It's fascinating to me that some educators show concern for—and even challenge—Hobsonville's modern approach. I always read this concern as an example of a fixed mindset challenging a growth mindset. Those few that challenge Hobsonville's methods do so from the standpoint that their conventional approach is somehow set in stone and does not require review. To this, Maurie says, "Others talk about us using students as guinea pigs and having teething problems. (I hope we always have teething problems!)"[13]

---

12 "Principal Possum: Hobsonville Point Secondary School ..." 2014. 27 Feb. 2016, http://principalpossum.blogspot.co.nz/2014/02/hobsonville-point-secondary-school.html

13 Teething problems are problems that you experience in the early stages of an activity.

After all, are not all teachers trying new things to improve learning for their students, and thus all learners exist in part as "guinea pigs" at whichever school they attend? I would be far more concerned to find a classroom not trying anything new. It's the very fact that the Hobsonville students are consulted and expected to be significant players in the development of learning at the school that makes it such an empowering environment for all.

One of the things that drives the philosophy at Hobsonville is a wish to maintain in its students a desire to grow and learn. Maurie points out that the New Zealand educational review office (ERO) that monitors and reports on each school's practice noted in a student well-being report:

> *In all 60+ secondary schools it looked at for its report, "the key factor was that students in all schools were experiencing an assessment-driven curriculum and assessment anxiety," and "In many schools the only people who understood the overall curriculum and the competing demands on them were the students."[14]*

This is why it seems obvious to involve students in the shaping of their own learning. Otherwise schools lose sight of what a year at school is really like for their students. The mindset held by the staff at this school means there is nothing to prohibit each year starting with adjusted aims, timetables, and learning structures. But all this reflection and change makes for a far more dynamic place of learning with all involved seen as equally qualified to make suggestions. Students are asked for "their views on any major decisions we are going to make."[15] This learner-centric approach is evident in Maurie's comments on the often-constraining task of timetabling:

---

14 "Findings - Education Review Office." 2015. 11 May 2016,
  http://www.ero.govt.nz/National-Reports/Wellbeing-for-
  Young-People-s-Success-at-Secondary-School-February-2015/
  Findings
15 "Principal Possum: Slow Learning." 2015. 28 Feb. 2016,
  http://principalpossum.blogspot.co.nz/2015/09/slow-learning.html

I have grown to love the elegance of timetabling—not timetabling as I once knew it, when the concentration was on creating an administratively efficient machine that looked remarkably like last year's and contained the same type of "acceptable restrictions" as in previous years, which required a shoe horn to force every one of our learners into! Such a timetable always resulted in comments such as, "I'd really like to do that, but the timetable won't let me!" I'm embarrassed to say that I've uttered that tragic line in the past to either quell my own crazy ideas or to dismiss the crazy innovative thoughts of others. The timetabling I've grown to love is one that subjugates the timetable to its role of representing the vision and values of the school and bringing life to the curriculum design principles that emerge from the vision and values—a timetable that is flexible and responsive with the needs of the learner firmly at the centre.[16]

Rather than see this as a softening of approach in comparison to the more formal, conventional way of schooling, I believe this method demands far more of the students. They must not only complete the work, but also justify what, why, and how they will learn, and then present this to others. Maurie says, "We ask them to identify which contexts they would like to explore their learning in, and we ask them to suggest the best ways for them to process their learning and the best ways to evidence their learning."

A common phrase at Hobsonville Point High School is, "Be warm and demanding." Teachers implement a "critical friend" system for all staff. This creates a buddy system where practice is expected to be challenged by a colleague in a friendly fashion. Something that might scare many teachers in other schools is that one of the Hobsonville teachers has to be the principal's critical friend and ensure his practice as leader is challenged. I find this particularly impressive, as this is a

---

16 "Principal Possum: It's Not Only The Kids Who Learn Here!" 2015. 28 Feb. 2016, http://principalpossum.blogspot.com/2015/05/danger-super-heroes-at-work-i-have.html

professional expectation that I know many schools would struggle to implement because the school's culture is not in a trusting position to do so.

The irony for me is that schools like Hobsonville represent what New Zealand education has been trying to encourage in its schools for more than a decade. It's nice to see we are getting there but disappointing to know there are still many school leaders using their autonomy to cling to conventional models of high schooling that actually are no longer encouraged by any of the official values, key competencies, or documentation. Maurie states the following on leading change:

> On reflecting on leadership I have experienced in schools in the past, I realised most leadership was about managing the status quo (hardly an inspirational imperative for leadership). Then things changed a little so leaders had to now "manage change," as if it were an inconvenience that were disrupting the status quo. Change can't be managed, especially rapid change. Managing something means dealing with it when it's here and now so it is quite reactive. I came to the conclusion that leading for the future requires us to lead change.[17]

It is within a regular high school community that Hobsonville and its teachers are doing extraordinary things. In the next section, I thought I would showcase additional examples of leadership and learning that takes place in the context of challenging circumstances.

---

17 "Principal Possum: Leadership, Moral Purpose and Courage." 2015. 28 Feb. 2016, http://principalpossum.blogspot.co.nz/2015/03/leadership-moral-purpose-and-courage.html

Kia Aroha High School, Principal Dr. Ann Milne
kiaaroha.school.nz

I heard Ann speak at New Zealand's main education conference, ULearn. She had a large audience, and I could see from the Twitter backchannel as she spoke that she was inspiring many, not in how her school was using tech or some special new pedagogy, but something far more important. Ann is the principal of Kia Aroha College, a high school in south Auckland. This school serves a community classed as one of the poorest in New Zealand. The challenges they face as a school outnumber and outsize those faced by most schools. So how does Ann tackle these head on? I would sum it up as a combination of community engagement, genuine respect for the culture, individual identity of every learner, and the development of self-respect as the main themes of her approach.

When she started talking, I thought New Zealand was doing a fabulous job of fully respecting Māori and Pacific Island cultures. But early on in her presentation, Ann made it very clear that a large chasm still exists between our curriculum aims and the schools' and ministry of education's attempts to deliver on them.

Kia Aroha College's Learning Model is outlined as follows:
- Learning is integrated—across subject areas and with students' lives and realities.
- Learning is negotiated—by students, with teachers.
- Learning is inquiry-based and student driven.
- Learning is critical—it provides young people with the power and the tools to understand and challenge inequity and injustice and to make change in their lives.
- Learning is whānau-based—it is collective, cooperative, collaborative, and reciprocal, i.e., learning is shared: you receive it, you share it, you give back to other learners.

- Learning is based in strong relationships—with self, with each other, with teachers, with the learning itself and its relevance, with the world beyond school and between home and school.
- Learning is culturally located and allows you to live your cultural norms throughout the school day.

What's inspiring here is that Kia Aroha College achieves what is often described as a modern learning model by implementing what is actually recognised by them as an extremely traditional, community-based, and common sense approach to developing young people. There seems little need for the school to discuss modern learning environments or personalised learning because their approach pays extra focus to the personal culture and community of every individual. The school has used a genuine focus on the individual to successfully move on from the industrial one-size-fits-all educational model that the rest of the developed world is busy dragging itself away from.

It was great to see, in 2015, further national recognition for new approaches to education when the New Zealand Principals' Federation issued Ann a Service with Distinction Award for being a member "who has made an outstanding contribution to the teaching profession or education as a principal." This is yet another example of how the various authorities that combine to operate education in New Zealand are aligned in recognising the need for flexible approaches to suit individual learners' needs.

To better appreciate the polar opposite of one-size-fits-all education, I highly recommend checking out Kia Aroha College's website: http://www.kiaaroha.school.nz/. I hope when you read this that the school website still opens with their welcoming video, as it will give you a real sense of how the strong cultural aspect of living in New Zealand creates a respect for differences.

Questions for Readers

1. How aware are the teachers you know of their local schools that are leading in pedagogy?

2. How collaborative are your local schools in sharing best practice and ideas?

3. What evidence do you have that your school is overtly supporting an individual's right to be and express themselves as they are?

Chapter 8
Culture: Formal Education in Tolerance and Respect

E ven the most serious issues in a society can be systematically addressed by its education system. To be clear, New Zealand has not solved or completely eliminated issues around race, culture, and tolerance, but the initiatives it has implemented as integral parts of its education have made a serious start at addressing these concerns.

This chapter is about aspirations, perseverance, and progress on a national scale in addressing difficulties that are common the world over. There are many things I love about New Zealand's education system, but none inspire me more than what educators are doing and expected to do regarding our official bicultural status. In a world of terrorism and racial tensions, the young people of New Zealand are being introduced to a more tolerant world as part of their education. When you see hashtags such as #Syria or #BlackLivesMatter, or see the horrors people experience in many parts of the world, rich and poor, due to ignorance and prejudice, you realise that education has a duty to overtly tackle tolerance and acceptance as fundamental to improving the lives of millions.

The challenge for education is to ensure all teachers are encouraged and supported to develop their learners' empathy towards and understanding of cultural differences. New Zealand's need to educate learners in its bicultural status has meant that cultural awareness is an issue that arises daily at all age levels and in all subject specialisms. The requirement to show appreciation for and a growth in understanding of Māori culture, language, and customs, within a teacher's classroom methods and communicating with the school community, is taken seriously enough that it forms part of their renewed practicing certificate process every three years.

How Culture Shapes Education—and Vice Versa

The founding of New Zealand is centred on the signing of the Treaty of Waitangi. This was the treaty between the colonial British and the indigenous Māori tribes. Like many treaty signings in history, this one, too, is clouded in controversy. In brief terms, the British duped the Māori people into handing over most of New Zealand's land. This has led to nearly 200 years of various types of disputes, including war, and some of these are still in the courts, although most issues around ownership are now settled with much being returned to the Māori people.

A national feeling of guilt and a need to recognise the vast history and importance of the Māori people to New Zealand's identity has led to a formalised recognition of Māori customs and beliefs in most aspects of our culture, including government, medicine, and education. The difficulties in reconciling the relationship between Māori and Pakeha (Māori for non-Māori) is the reason education in this country requires a direct approach to ensuring that future generations are aware of the important differences and priorities held by each culture. The hope is that such awareness would build a positive relationship and a better country.

The primary example of this recognition in education was the formation of two distinctly different curriculums, either of which any school can choose. This is not simply an English-language curriculum and translation into Māori but a full reworking of how the same values and goals might be realised within Māori context and customs. Coming from the United Kingdom with its strict lists of mandated content, it was fascinating for me to see how New Zealand had embraced both cultures. More than anything I had seen or experienced to date, the country's willingness to create a dual-curriculum emphasised to me, as an outsider, that it valued a learner's individual circumstances and background.

The intentionality of New Zealanders toward recognising differences in culture has the effect of honouring the importance of relationships. One way this is modelled is through making the debate over how cultures can work together part of the normal conversation. It's an attitude that has an impact on all of the elements and processes within education, which is possibly a big driver behind the development of a focus on skills over content.

Having culturally sensitive curriculums that are free from prescribed content is one of the most futuristic aspects of New Zealand education. Allowing schools to tailor learning and its priorities to the cultural sensitivities of their communities, and of the individual, is key to developing in students a true, intrinsic motivation to learn. The conventional factory-style education system applied in most countries has always ignored an individual's circumstance and experiences. Thus, millions of students around the world feel alienated from what should be an authentic and personal learning experience. The crux of the matter is that people must feel comfortable in the context in which they are learning.

Let's take a look at how these two curriculums differ and show respect to a positive attitude towards cultural differences.

Two Official but Very Different Curriculums

One of the key reasons our high school assessment is so flexible and accommodating to multiple learning approaches is that it effectively *has* to for legal reasons. In an attempt to show full appreciation for our bicultural status, we have two full curriculums available for any school to choose to adopt, whether they are predominantly Māori or Pakeha (non-Māori). As I mentioned, the difference in the curriculum is not just about language translation, but about values, beliefs, and customs that influence how an individual might learn and best experience formal education.

Te Marautanga o Aotearoa (the Māori curriculum) takes an entirely different approach to not only the content but also the priorities for learning. I am not going to pretend to be an expert in Māori curriculum, but the important thing to point out (lest anyone thinks the dual-curriculum is the result of political correctness gone mad) is that the students who receive learning based on the Māori curriculum are measured for high school graduation with the same standards and assessments. These assessments will be moderated against any that are issued by a New Zealand Curriculum school. The only difference is the approach schools using Te Marautanga o Aotearoa take to achieve the same confident and skilled learners. The aim is to deliver all of life's fundamental skills and knowledge through practices that respect and support the history, culture, and spiritual side of Māori existence. This doesn't mean that students of Te Marautanga o Aotearoa miss out on anything. What's particularly impressive is that, like the New Zealand curriculum, the Māori curriculum is meant to be treated as a framework from which schools build local curriculums. The aim is for schools to develop a curriculum that respects the needs and priorities of the local *iwi* (tribe) and community.

Language

When trying to maintain cultural tolerance and respect, something history reveals can be lost quite easily, it seems to me that having daily exposure to both official languages appears to have a positive normalising effect on cultural acceptance amongst the population. In New Zealand, radio and TV news and weather reports make a special effort to start and end reports with Māori greetings and use proper pronunciation of all the Māori named towns and cities. In fact, it's funny when you see two generations of New Zealanders, such as a five-year-old and a fifty-year-old talking about the same place but with different pronunciations. For example, many European colonial descendants who have been in New Zealand from before the 1990s will say Taupo as "Tow-poe" but every five-year-old brought up on the proper pronunciation will correctly say "Toe-paw."

Schools also adopt a regular use of the language in the classroom and during official events. Teachers' practising certificate requirements also demand evidence of Māori language use in the classroom, regardless of whether or not they teach Māori students. The belief is that the Māori language is an important part of any New Zealander's identity.

A fantastic display of Māori culture that also shows a general respect for others is the performance of *waiatas* when welcoming visitors to schools. After formal Māori welcomes, staff from the host school, often comprising the principal and leadership team, will perform a Māori song to welcome the guests, and then the visitors themselves will stand and sing a returning *waiata*. These songs are to represent each tribe's values, and I've seen on many occasions parents of performing students standing and joining in from their seats in the audience. It's a wonderful way to start any ceremony, including, for example, our national education conferences.

National Identity

When I am talking to students of any race or background about the importance of learning Māori language and culture, I use it as the local and very tangible example of why learning any language and culture can be as practically useful and career focused as any subject covered by schools. Although our history with Māori cultural understanding and acceptance is checkered, it has always been used as a draw card to foreigners and tourists. As an example, a Māori rugby team toured England as far back as 1905, as a showpiece for the country. Our education system has a duty to reflect the important role that Māori culture plays in the identity of our relatively new country.

On a more practical level, learning the Māori language and culture, like learning any second language, offers students thousands of career opportunities. In a world where language learning in developed countries is experiencing a downturn, and where cultural misunderstanding is leading to negative—even disastrous—consequences, the compulsory requirement for all New Zealand students to regularly learn about and experience another culture offers hope for a better, more inclusive society.

Questions for Readers

1. What is your education system doing to systematically and successfully tackle tolerance and prejudice?

2. What would a formally recognised approach to education in cultural tolerance and understanding look like in your country?

Chapter 9
New Zealand Teacher Practising Certificate—Encouraging Growth, Not Competency

In an education system run by schools and students, you can imagine the public's need for reassurance that the teachers will do the right things to maintain high standards. The practising certificate process that I've mentioned a few times thus far has a great deal to do with ensuring students get the best possible education.

In most countries, once you've qualified as a teacher, you can then relax. As long as you don't do anything too silly, you'll maintain a happy (possibly stressful) teaching career. This is not the case in New Zealand. Teachers must renew their practising certificate as a New Zealand educator every three years. That seems like a lot of work, but trust me, it's not. The expectation is that teachers record some of their excellent work in a portfolio (commonly a blog) as an on-going project. The key point to remember here is this recertification is not simply a case of proving yourself against a fixed list of good teacher competencies. Remember, New Zealand doesn't do "fixed." No, this is a personalised expectation that teachers consider and record their growth in twelve criteria for teaching professionals. As long as there is growth, you're doing the right thing.

Am I Being Judged?

When mentoring new teachers at my school, I explain that they should regularly record the new initiatives and best moments that happen in their teaching. Anytime they try something new or see great results, they need to record it—not simply for their next practising certificate review, but also so those results can be shared for the benefit of colleagues and teachers around New Zealand.

You might now be wondering how collected evidence is judged for certification. The Education Council is a division of the ministry that was created specifically to maintain excellence in the teaching profession. The council includes teachers, and it monitors and checks the practising certificate process using twelve categories for growth it expects to see from each teacher. But remember, this process is not as simple as ticking off boxes on a teacher competency list.

Looking for Growth Promotes Learning

The reason I think the practising certificate process is essential to a good education system is that it promotes the idea of lifelong learning through its educators. The judgements are not made by confirming evidence of the twelve criteria simply taking place within a classroom. What the council and school leaders look for is evidence of growth in each of the twelve areas since the educator was last certified. It's about growth, not competency. The question asked in appraisals is not, "Are you a competent teacher?" but "How are you better than you were three years ago?"

This practising certificate initiative was introduced before the new curriculum, but like the curriculum document, has taken a few years for school leaders and teachers to understand that it is a positive thing and not a negative or judgemental initiative. You might understand that issuing teaching practising certificates on only a temporary basis would instigate bad feelings amongst members of the profession. I have more recently witnessed that with the growth of education's connected community, especially online, there is a new mindset towards these growth criteria. The willingness to record, reflect on, and even promote what one does in the classroom simply makes sense in a world of blogs and social media. And the comfort most new teachers have with blogging and sharing online makes selling the system to them relatively easy, especially if they have a growth mindset.

The twelve criteria offer the appraisal process a simple list of important and aspirational requirements if you are to develop as an educator. As they are compulsory, every educator can be expected each year to identify three or four new teaching initiatives on which to focus, so as to collect the required evidence by the end of the three-year cycle. The requirements make the appraisal process feel less judgemental and more objective and goal oriented.

Here's a summary of the twelve criteria that are used to ensure all teachers are having conversations and reflecting on the important growth areas for educators:

New Zealand Teacher Practising Certificate Criteria

Professional Relationships and Professional Values[1]

1. Establish and maintain effective professional relationships focused on the learning and well-being of all ākonga (learners).

    a. This is evidence of new connections made with other teachers, schools, parents, and communities for the benefit of learning. Showing evidence of new connections made during the past three years is critical to being an effective educator.

---

1   "Practising Teacher Criteria | Education Council." 2016. 29 May 2016, https://educationcouncil.org.nz/content/practising-teacher-criteria-0

2. Demonstrate commitment to promoting the well-being of all äkonga (learners).

   a. This is evidence of new ideas a teacher might have implemented to better cater to every student's needs. For me, it's like having a Universal Design for Learning (UDL) category. "UDL provides a blueprint for creating instructional goals, methods, materials, and assessments that work for everyone—not a single, one-size-fits-all solution, but rather flexible approaches that can be customized and adjusted for individual needs."[2]

3. Demonstrate commitment to bicultural partnership in Aotearoa New Zealand.

   a. It is a requirement that a teacher's practice shows genuine appreciation for the customs and mindset of the Mäori people. This includes promoting these customs and mindsets to all learners we are educating. The approach towards learning and priorities for Mäori differ from that of the colonial European culture and must be recognised. Mäori culture is heavily centred on appreciating whanau (extended family/tribe). The culture also has its own spiritual understandings and stories. The Mäori approach must be available as options to every child in every classroom. Mäori, in particular, must be allowed to succeed as Mäori.

4. Demonstrate commitment to ongoing professional learning and development of personal professional practice.

   a. This specifically refers to being involved in professional development including that which is provided by the school.

---

2   "What UDL is - National Center On Universal Design for Learning." 2009. 29 May 2016, http://www.udlcenter.org/aboutudl/whatisudl

5. Show leadership that contributes to effective teaching and learning.

   a. Evidence of leading initiatives within schools is required. This might be simply sharing a new teaching idea with colleagues.

Professional Knowledge in Practice

6. Conceptualise, plan, and implement an appropriate learning programme.

   a. This might seem like the nuts and bolts of teaching but does allow a teacher's manager, be that the principal or faculty manager, to hold teachers to account for how much they contribute to the learning that takes place in a school or department. As a leader in a school, I'm able to use this criterion to push those teachers who expect to be handed the material and script to deliver.

7. Promote a collaborative, inclusive, and supportive learning environment.

   a. Notice here that a New Zealand learning environment promotes collaboration as its first indicator. This criteria always makes me think of those classic individual desks you find in most American classrooms that physically restrict group work. New Zealand hasn't issued individual student desks for thirty years! As a leader, I have found this criteria very useful to challenge teachers on the need to be flexible about how they manage the classroom. If it is to be truly inclusive of every student's needs, it must be flexible, social, and collaborative. This is, after all, how the best learning takes place.

8. Demonstrate in practice their knowledge and understanding of how ākonga[3] learn.

   a. This, again, points to flexibility in approach to learning and also gives teachers a need to keep abreast with pedagogical ideas. Remember that teachers are expected to show growth, and so with new educational theory moving forward, they will be expected to show awareness of and inquiries into current good practice.

9. Respond effectively to the diverse language and cultural experiences and the varied strengths, interests, and needs of individuals and groups of ākonga (learners).

   a. Consider this: A legal demand from the country that every teacher personalises learning and then grows in their ability to do so. I love the fact that this can only be demanded of all teachers because it is possible even at the very senior end of high school graduation assessment.

10. Work effectively within the bicultural context of Aotearoa New Zealand.

   a. This might sound like criteria three and has caused confusion. However, put simply, it refers to the teacher's own practice in their use of Māori custom and language. Rather than what the learners are doing, this looks at how the teacher responds to ideas and events in a manner appropriate to Māori expectations. The goal of this, again, is to benefit the bicultural experience and education of all students, not just Māori.

11. Analyse and appropriately use assessment information, which has been gathered formally and informally.

   a. Mark Quigley, a colleague of mine, pointed out to the staff at my school that so much of what happens in

---

3 Ākonga means student or learner

education is based on "gut feeling." Educators who use data properly and objectively frequently discover new information about their students, information that may not be obvious in the busy classroom. The data might reveal such things as, for example, a relational issue with a student when you analyse their school results to discover they only underperform in your class (this has happened to me). It's critical that teachers keep in mind how they develop their use of data, and the teacher certification process helps teachers reflect on how they are improving their use of available data.

12. Use critical inquiry and problem-solving effectively in their professional practice.

    a.   This is my favourite of all twelve. To formally expect and hold all teachers accountable for reflection and inquiry into their practice is something that helps New Zealand keep forward momentum. Too few teachers, in my experience, systematically reflect and challenge their own practices, relying instead on gut feelings rather than evidence. As a leader who appraises teachers, this criteria allows us to examine how teachers are looking into the profession and into their own practices. This is very much the criteria for developing a growth mindset across the whole profession.

The teacher practising certificate is an important tool to keep extremely busy teachers reflective about the excellent work they do. Many teachers now use blogs and electronic portfolios to record the evidence and reflections. This itself has encouraged more teachers into blogging, sharing, and connecting and has created a great source of professional development materials for many.

Questions for Readers

1. Would you, as a teacher, feel threatened by the twelve criteria listed above?

2. Does the idea of renewing practising certificates every three years seem like a positive idea?

3. What systems does your school use to keep teachers reflective on their practice?

Chapter 10
I'm Not Kiwi; What Can I Do?

N ow I do understand that it's quite likely you do not live in New Zealand. If that's the case, you may be thinking that these ideas presented from the New Zealand Curriculum are all very good but can't be replicated in other contexts.

But they can.

In fact, it's possible to implement future-focused education, even within restrictive, test-driven education systems. You simply have to find creative ways to make the learning student-centred and student-driven. The ideas that follow are all based on my own experiences, be that in my teaching practice or through school visits, and I believe they can be incorporated in almost any classroom.

Flipped Teaching: Remove the Test from the Classroom

Until 2012, I was still predominantly teaching high school students a fixed, predetermined curriculum and preparing them for three-hour exams on the content. This was because I had come from the United Kingdom and found myself working in a private school, whose academic point of difference from the public system was to offer the GCSE and A-level exam system. Between seeing Ken Robinson's TED Talk in 2006 and leaving for a public school in 2012, I had become skilled in the art of avoiding teaching the exam material and attempting to personalise every student's experience. You see, it is my view that teaching exam material to a class does not work. Tests cannot meet each individual's needs for learning; it is a practice that should simply be stopped. This started with a big smile on my face as I announced a statement to the class at the beginning of the 2012 school year: "I will NOT teach the class anything for the exams."

I went on to explain that all exam material would be flipped into five-minute videos. These videos would be the only class-wide instruction available. During 2011, I had worked through my normal teaching schedule recording the five-minute videos one week ahead. What alarmed my colleagues—and anyone I've met since—is that, when videoed into concise, edited, and animated videos, any high school year-thirteen (K12) annual course material is delivered in under four hours. I was working in a boys' school at the time, and typical for teenage boys, many spent the year doing personal projects in app development and only occasionally watched the exam videos. A night or two before the exams, all the boys crammed by using the videos, running through the entire content delivered by me in four hours. Results rose steeply from that year on, with me making minor improvements to the videos in following years. The question I asked myself was, "What does it mean for learning when all students can get great results cramming all exam content into four hours? How can we judge those young people in terms of being useful citizens from an A grade that took four hours of study?"

The irony here is that successfully flipping my content made life much easier for me, whilst it put me off standardised curriculums even further. Thankfully, I had the option to "jump ship" and get away from standardised testing since New Zealand offered me an alternative approach to teaching.

Reduce Teacher Dependence in Your Classroom

One complaint I've heard from teachers at both the elementary and high school levels is that generally, kids are needy. Most teachers still work in a constant loop of the same questions:

- What are we doing today?
- Where do you want us to start?
- What should we use for this?
- Where do we find the answers?
- How long have we got?

Students around the world are conditioned every day by schools to expect the structure and format of each moment to be decided for them. Add to this timetables and bells that instruct students to be in certain rooms for certain timeslots, and you realise that the level of experience in being independent and self-organising is minimal—skills that are critical on the first day, pre-high school. No wonder teachers, and adults in general, get frustrated by or joke about how needy and lacking in intuition young people are.

Five Questions to Remove from Your Classroom

I talk about teaching and learning quite a lot. In fact, if you ask my wife, probably a little too much. Because of this, teachers in my department ask me questions about what I want them to be aiming for and what suggestions I have for the classes. Rather than spend too much time talking about pedagogy and teaching models, I try to keep it simple and look at the language the students are using in the classroom.

I could go into a lengthy discussion now about deep thinking and *unGoogleable* questions, but let's keep it simple. Here are five questions I am aiming to never hear in my classroom, ever again. If these questions pop up, then they point to some fairly simple issues that can be solved with a combination of resources, technology, and new pedagogical ideas centred on empowering the learners. Here are the questions:

1. What are we doing today?

This question is a flag that indicates dependent students. Students who ask this question believe that learning is something that should be delivered by an external entity. The attitude behind it assumes learning is an organised event that one attends.

Your classroom must build an understanding that learning is constant. It must use approaches that encourage intrinsic desire to grow and take control of one's own learning. Make sure your questions are accessible and build habits in students to look after their own learning progress.

2. What do I do next?

No learning has an endpoint, which is why teachers need to develop a classroom culture based on an attitude of "How far can we take this?" rather than "Is there another predetermined step?" I encourage teachers to consider the difference between developing growth or fixed mindsets.

Growth feedback example: "You succeeded because you worked hard."

Fixed feedback example: "You succeeded because you're smart."

When students reach a dead end, teachers need to encourage open collaboration with peers to look for other options. This is critical to developing a culture of "we can" rather than "I can't."

3. Is this on the test?

I want to get something off my chest: all tests are a waste of time. There is no correlation between exam success and usefulness to a community or workplace. My advice for teachers locked in education systems centred on testing is to flip the teaching and get on with proper learning. Negotiate collaborative projects with your students and present any test or exam as a separate issue, dealt with by video and individual teacher support afforded by the reduction in teaching delivery time.

4. Which app should I use?

Here's the best answer a teacher can give to this question:

"I'm not sure; try to find one," or

"Does it need an app?"

It's a sad moment and indication of poor learner mindset when a so-called digital native relies on tech answers from their born-before-the-Internet teachers. Very few young people in 2016 would do this outside the classroom, so a teacher has work to do if this question is reserved just for the school environment.

5. Is this good enough?

One aim I promote to teachers is to have students care about their work but NOT care what the teacher's opinion is. I've done much work with student-designed mark schemes (grading standards). I end most project units with a week of peer marking, where each group discusses what they would look for in a successful project; they then design the mark sheet. This makes the students consider every aspect of what they have done. It also encourages all involved to think about how any element could be improved. Most importantly, it starts to develop a genuine interest in the quality of their work, separate from what the teacher thinks.

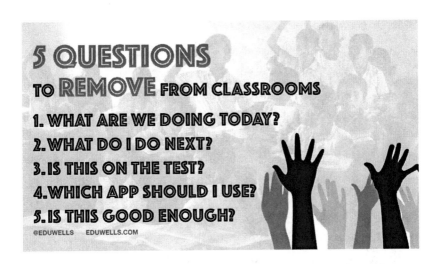

A Further Thought

The classroom is a strange environment, certainly unlike anything outside school. I really think teachers can do quiet harm by developing an environment where, because the teacher decides the path and provides direct help towards achieving predetermined goals, students become dependent on school structures. A teacher may get great results, but have they produced a classroom of school-ready or life-ready citizens?

Share Yourself to Grow Yourself

Hey, Teacher, are you aware of how magical you are? Make your practice visible to find out.

So there it was, a small middle school at the bottom of the world, filled with teachers and students who were just doing their thing. I visited the school on a research project funded by CORE Education in New Zealand. The school's leadership and learners were proud of what they were doing, but the issue for me was that "their thing" was MIND-BLOWING and nobody knew about it!

I wrote about this school in chapter seven. When I blogged about what I saw at this school,[1] I introduced the world to the learning approach taken by Breens Intermediate school. All I did was draw a diagram that loosely outlined what the school was doing. To quote a Californian, that blog went "absolutely VIRAL"!

USA, France, Finland, Canada, Sweden, Australia, Turkey, United Kingdom, public schools, private schools, elementary schools, high schools—you name it, they were interested. Above is an image containing just some of the messages, and it only includes those who quoted the Tweet—not the thousands of Retweets, likes, and re-blogging that occurred.

World-renowned educators and school principals were promising rethinks and planning sessions based on this school's methods, and teachers talked of dreaming about such a school or wanting to "go back to school" just to experience it. I was humbled by the response but at the same time not surprised. But what does this mean?

---

1 "Hey teacher, would YOU be a student? – @EDUWELLS." 2015. 9 Apr. 2016, http://eduwells.com/2015/11/21/hey-teacher-would-you-be-a-student/

Share It to Discover Your Own Awesomeness!

Breens is special but not unique. It is one more example of something that can happen in every school: a GREAT IDEA. Nearly all schools and teachers are doing great things, the issue is that they don't know they're great until they share them, and this is not happening enough. If you are an educator, I promise you that "thing" you are doing right now in school would be mind-blowing to thousands of teachers. By not sharing it, you are underestimating the potential impact your idea could have on the world of education.

21st CENTURY SCHOOL IN 20th CENTURY BUILDINGS

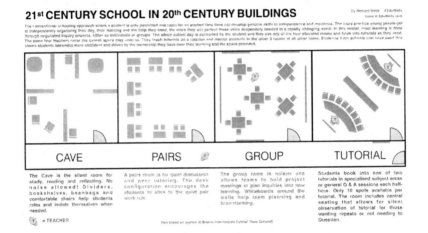

We Think in Pictures

There's another important reason why my post was popular: pictures! Humans like pictures. We think in pictures and need them to process ideas properly. The graphic I produced was carefully arranged, used colour and layout to divide information, and was easy to spot and digest. This is important for all teachers and school leaders to be aware of when promoting new initiatives.

Scared to Share?

I also know that some teachers simply refuse to share their ideas and results. My research shows that unconnected educators were not comfortable sharing because of professional uncertainty about their practice. Until you've shared and gained your first feedback, you are unable to position yourself on a sort of educators' "success spectrum." Until you bounce your ideas off someone else, you can't judge the response they may receive. Regardless of how confident you are, I have a solution: draw and share as a school.

Make sure your school has a Twitter account. (Twitter is the primary social media for educators.) Ask your teachers to submit their latest classroom ideas and initiatives and promote them as a school to the world using #EdChat and #EdTech. This takes the pressure off the individuals, whilst promoting what probably will be AWESOME educational gold to schools around the globe. Start today, or I'll hunt down your amazing ideas and do it for you!

Why New Zealand Schools Are Turning to Student-Centric Learning

A recent job vacancy for a leadership position in a New Zealand school asked for a focus on genuine student-centred learning. What fascinated me was their use of the word *genuine*. Experience shows us that confusion, misinterpretation, and a lack of exposure to relevant examples means that too many educators do not understand true student-centric learning. Many schools feel under pressure to be implementing such models, but often only change surface-level elements whilst proclaiming they have achieved it.

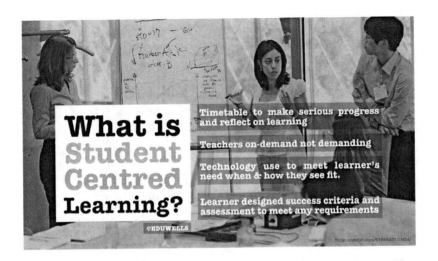

Why Being Student-Centric Matters

Let's cut to the chase. Being student-centric matters because we all know that young people (including ourselves many moons ago) would rather stay at home than go to school. If students tell people they like school, what they're often picturing as they say it are things such as hangin' with friends, music productions, or the sports events. When students are asked what their favourite part of school is, they rarely mention anything that takes place in a classroom. I recently asked three boys, who had moved from elementary to junior high, what was positive about the change. They actually agreed on "moving between rooms" as the first improvement that sprung to mind. That's right, folks—their best part of the daily school experience is the brief time spent chatting in the corridor! All you have to do is endure an hour with one teacher and then you get a break for five minutes before the next.

The New Zealand education review office that runs quality assurance checks on schools' practice recently reported that in sixty-eight schools, "Students in all schools were experiencing an assessment-driven curriculum and assessment anxiety. In many schools the only people who understood the overall curriculum and the competing demands on them were the students."[2]

The constant amongst most schools that drives this pessimistic view is that students rarely control any significant part of their day. As an example of how common this view is, I can even use teachers to prove my point. I've worked in four schools that have all held teacher training days. During a number of those days, sessions have been prearranged to showcase tools or pedagogies, and staff have moved from one session to another. Many of these days have received feedback that they were not very useful. A recent example I experienced broke the trend and offered longer sessions of self-directed time for colleagues from the same department to work on their own material. The feedback included:

> "Best staff training days so far. We got to work on our own stuff and had time to get things done. It was great to work with other departments."

Many teachers agree that student-directed learning makes sense when it comes to their own learning, but this rarely translates to their approach to teaching. Releasing control is always difficult, so I thought I'd do my best to outline some practical questions and advice from my own experience that will hopefully make some teachers reconsider their need for absolute control of when, what, and how learning takes place.

1. Time(table) to Learn.

Timetabling the day has more impact than you think: How the day is divided often shapes its potential to engage people in learning. A comment by a New Zealand principal has confused many educators to whom I've shown it:

---

2 "Wellbeing for Young People's Success at Secondary School. February ..." 2016. 29 May 2016, http://www.ero.govt.nz/assets/Uploads/ERO-Wellbeing-SecondSchools-web.pdf

"The timetabling I've grown to love is that which subjugates the timetable to its role of representing the vision and values of the school and bringing life to the curriculum design principles that emerge from the vision and values—a timetable that is flexible and responsive with the needs of the learner firmly at the centre." —Maurie Abraham (NZ Principal)

The idea of a timetable representing the vision for the school confuses many people. The way you allocate time indicates your priorities and thus your values. Teachers who are accustomed to a day centred on their needs don't view the timetable as an enabler for students to learn but as another mechanism for managing them.

One major requirement for learning is reflection. Hardly any schools timetable for it.

"We do not learn from experience ... we learn from reflecting on experience." —John Dewey

Students are normally given no time to reflect on recent learning before they are thrown into another unrelated lesson (high school) or topic (elementary).

2. Release Control.

If your timetable is focused on the needs of the learners rather than teachers, then you'll be free to let the students shape a great deal of your day. One issue that both restricts student experience and makes it less engaging is that the whole day is often prearranged by the teachers for the teachers. Where to be, what to look at, and what to aim for has been predicted and so actually demands less challenge. Learning happens best when the learner is immersed in the experience. To truly immerse, a learner must have input into that experience.

Compliance is not learning, even if it results in good grades. Teachers should arrive at work wondering how they will be needed, not how students will conform to their pre-arrangements. I've always thought that the prescribed experience school teachers themselves experienced in the twentieth century is to blame for so many not taking ownership of their own professional development. Many are still waiting for the imaginary professional development timetable and activities to be written for them. I wouldn't want to think we were breeding another generation of people who wait for learning to be arranged.

3. Allow Technology to Achieve its Potential.

Technology is not essential, but it helps. A large number of schools are now using technology, but teachers' prearranged learning and goals restrict the experience for students in what potential there is to explore and discover with technology and the Internet. Rather than learn, they are asked to use technology to achieve prearranged targets. This does not allow them to experience the same real learning process that people do outside classrooms.

Most young people are used to exploring and contributing to online discussion and events in their personal lives. Many schools don't make the most of this activity and create an abstract environment where study material has already been sorted and the path a discussion will follow has been well trodden by previous classes. Access to technology should be an empowering opportunity, and I hope teachers ask students to surprise them with what they can achieve rather restrict expectations with rigidly structured tasks.

4. Students Owning Their Assessment

Involving students in the design of assessment is both crucial to engagement and is exactly what any learning involves when people outside schools undertake a challenge. If adults attempt to learn anything, they start by setting criteria for how they will know they've reached their goal, be it piano or a Google Chrome extension. This is also something we generally deny students in schools. They are normally adhering to someone else's idea of success. In doing this, teachers and schools remove an important personal connection to the learning experience.

I have experimented much in the last three years by challenging students to consider what marks success within each task they undertake. I have been surprised by how engaging this activity is for my students. It might be because it's a novelty in relation to other learning they do, but one group, for example, extended the assessment design to a full week of lessons without any encouragement from me!

Even if you are working in a high school where assessments are set by high authorities, ensure your students have time to review the course demands and construct their own list of requirements. To some teachers, this will seem like a waste of time when they have already done it for them. But again, I stress that it is part of true learning, and to remove this step only creates an environment of compliance in which the skill of learning is not developed by the students.

Like reflection, considering one's own success criteria is an important part of the learning process, and schools should reintroduce this if learning is ever to be considered as authentic and meaningful.

Put Your Vision into Action!

Many schools will state that they want students to be independent, responsible, and confident. But if your students are walking into a school environment where every aspect is prearranged, you remove the need to be independent, responsible, and confident about anything. We say practice makes progress; well let's start allowing students to practise what we want them to become.

Chapter 11
Let's End at the Beginning

I can't end a book on New Zealand education without highlighting that the hard work was done when the curriculum documents were created. The emphasis on learning and personal growth—for all, and not just the students—has created an education system that is charging ahead of others. Below is my visual summary of the core elements of our curriculum that includes my ideas on why these are so important. It is the only example I can find where I would say the horse is literally placed before the cart. It's the only example where any mention of subjects or content themes is found halfway into the document. Developing motivated learners of all ages across New Zealand is the aim, and the traditional success criteria such as exam and employment success will naturally follow for successful learners in the twenty-first century.

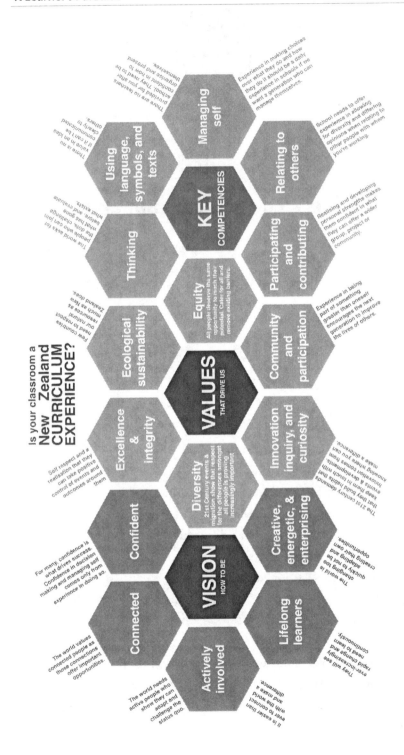

Is your classroom a
New Zealand
CURRICULUM
EXPERIENCE?

KEY COMPETENCIES

Managing self

Experience in making choices over what they do and how they do it should be a daily experience in schools if we want a generation who can manage themselves.

Thrive in no teachers provided for years after school. They need to be confident in how to organise in how to present themselves.

Using language, symbols, and texts

There is no value in an idea if it can't be communicated clearly to others.

Relating to others

School needs to offer experience in allowing for diversity and differing opinions when relating to other people with whom you're working.

Thinking

The world asks for people who can join the dots, challenge what has gone before, and evaluate what exists.

Participating and contributing

Realising and developing personal strengths makes them confident in what they can offer a wider group, project or community.

Ecological sustainability

Few countries need to respect our natural resource as much as New Zealand does.

Equity

All people deserve the same opportunity to reach their potential. Cater for all and remove existing barriers.

VALUES THAT DRIVE US

Community and participation

Experience in being part of something greater than oneself encourages the next generation to improve the lives of others.

Excellence & integrity

Self respect and a realisation that they can take positive control of events and outcomes around them

Diversity

21st Century events & migration show that respect for the differences amongst all people is proving increasingly important

Innovation, inquiry, and curiosity

The 21st century demands that they build habits that deep them in touch with events & developments. Innovation comes from knowing where you make a difference.

Confident

For many confidence is what drives success. Confidence in decision making and managing self comes only from experience in doing so.

VISION HOW TO BE

Creative, energetic, & enterprising

The world is changing too quickly to not be adapting and creating their own opportunities.

Connected

The world values connected people as those connections offer important opportunities

Actively involved

The world needs active people who show they can adapt and challenge the status quo.

It is easier than ever to connect with the world and make a difference.

Lifelong learners

They will see ever-increasingly rapid change and need to learn continuously.

Putting the Horse before the Cart

Most people assume formal education is a process of individual development from being heavily assisted at the age of five, moving on to only requiring guidance, and eventually achieving full independence and confidence to tackle one's own learning and growth. The sad truth is that most teachers of eighteen-year-olds will tell you that their students remain heavily dependent on constant guidance and support. I produced the graphic on the next page to sum up the three stages, and I wonder which one best depicts the average teenager in your education system.

Whether, as a teacher, you are tackling a prescribed set of content, have the luxury of devising your own, or even better, are negotiating the tasks and content with your students, it is worth considering who is doing most of the work. You can't develop a top footballer without allowing him or her to practise, try, fail, and try again. The same goes for what we want from our students. Most classrooms are so busy avoiding wrong answers they maintain and develop dependent learners who check with the teacher before making any step forward.

What Makes Students "Good"?

The top students in any school, through family, sporting, or performance experiences, are normally high achievers in spite of school and not because of it. They have arrived at the school having regularly experienced situations where their decision-making mattered; they were or remain responsible for the success of activities, and the possibility of failure was common. This is exactly the condition that the average school classroom avoids, and thus does not develop the average student into a genuinely motivated, confident citizen. At school, I was very much an average student and can confirm that any motivation and responsible decision-making was left until after university. I was kept safe from such matters by the education system I went through and spent my twenties working out how to perform effectively in teams and get projects completed on time.

PUTTING YOUR HORSE BEFORE THE CART

WHAT TYPE OF PERSON DOES YOUR CLASSROOM DEVELOP?

@EduWells

STUDENT
TEACHER

CLASSROOM A

A focus on the content (cart) means the teacher often retains the key competencies and self-esteem whilst remaining responsible for 50% of the learning progress all the way through education.

KNOWLEDGE & SKILLS

KEY COMPETENCIES

Result: Dependent Students

Many teachers of school leavers identify with this image as reflecting their classroom

CLASSROOM B

A focus on developing the student (horse) through independent learning experiences means the teacher becomes a guide whilst the student develops the needed self-esteem and competencies to tackle the content themselves.

LEARNING
SELF-GROWTH
KEY COMPETENCIES
SELF-ESTEEM

KNOWLEDGE & SKILLS

Result: Developing Students

CLASSROOM C

Like anything in life, independent, confident, and competent learners only eventuate from experience in being so. Only the one doing the work is learning. Let your students try & fail to truely succeed.

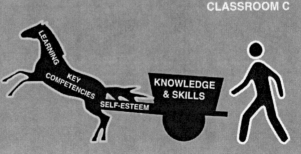

LEARNING
KEY COMPETENCIES
SELF-ESTEEM

KNOWLEDGE & SKILLS

Result: Independent, confident, citizens

"... But They Get the Grades!"

Please don't confuse success in exams and grade acquisition for genuine achievement. Many, if not most, top grades around the world are achieved through targeted teacher coaching—coaching only tuned for the specific prescribed challenges of the assessment at hand. This only results in what universities and employers report[1] as school leavers lacking initiative, motivation, and professional skills. This is not educational success by any stretch of the imagination. You will still get your grades if you devote time in early years to letting learners experience managing their own learning as a norm and not spoon-feeding content to them.

The Classroom Is for Developing People

The habit of many schools is to hand the responsibility of growing the person to extra-curricular activities and not the classroom, where the students spend most of their time. I can't tell you the number of times I've heard the words "all-round education" in discussion of sports or cultural events whilst at the same time the classroom is being reduced to only a place in which information is passed from teacher to student. Many adults make the mistake of thinking, "I went to school and turned out alright." But when challenged, they will conclude that any confidence or initiative they have was developed post-school, not during school. This I feel is a massive opportunity on which many non-high achievers miss out.

It's time to make the classroom as challenging as the sports field or theatre stage. Make the students more accountable for what takes place and whether or not it succeeds. Shift the responsibility from teacher to student for organising how the current challenges get tackled. It may go wrong initially but, like football players, they'll get better and better until they are ready to face their final school challenges independently.

---

1   "School leavers 'lack skills needed to get entry level jobs ..." 2014. 3 Apr. 2016, http://www.telegraph.co.uk/education/educationnews/10658100/School-leavers-lack-skills-needed-to-get-entry-level-jobs.html

It's Achievable—Play Safe and Start Early

This does not happen overnight. What I propose here is a vision for your school in five years' time, not tomorrow. Don't dismiss this because you can't picture your more senior students handling the responsibility of devising their own plans for learning. If they haven't had the prior practice, they're not going to take charge tomorrow. You have to build the expectations and competencies over a five-year process. Rethink the learning environments that your school's youngest learners experience, and let the current students live out the teacher-directed education they initially received as much as they need to. Focus on what your school will offer the next intake and how it will develop them to tackle the content without it being spoon-fed from Day One.

The Five-Year Progression

This type of plan for developing learners outlined in our national curriculum is what a growing number of schools are now focused on, or at least part of the way through. Most public schools have been through the introduction of "bring your own technology," and many are redesigning schools to shift the locus of control to the students.

Our national education resource website has pages dedicated to this shift in focus.[2]

Over to You, Wherever You Are

New Zealand is not absolute paradise yet, but we have the key components that will allow educators and learners to adapt as needed going forward.

I hope your education system is future focused. Even if it isn't, I hope you will choose to develop a mindset that challenges the status quo and considers how to best help your students become lifelong, independent learners. The point isn't to make students entirely independent of teachers but to instil in them the confidence to structure the learning in a way that suits their needs and interests. Be committed to guiding and ensuring their learning fits the requirements of the system and to mentoring them to realise the difference they can all make. Show them how they can achieve their personal best.

---

2   "Learning-focused relationships - Assessment - TKI." 2011. 3 Apr. 2016, http://assessment.tki.org.nz/Assessment-in-the-classroom/ Assessment-for-learning-in-practice/Learning-focused-relationships

Acknowledgments

I'd like to thank my endless list of inspiring Kiwi educators, especially those I've mentioned in the book. Special thanks go to Danielle Myburgh (@MissDtheTeacher), Steve Mouldey (@geomouldey) and Philippa Nicoll Antipas (@aKeenReader) for checking my ramblings and supporting all my efforts.

About the Author

Richard proudly started his career with an honours degree in Fine Art from Manchester in England. He worked in IT before getting contracted to work in schools, digitalising their workflows in the late 1990s. He became an educator in 2003 and after teaching and managing school departments for three years, moved to New Zealand in 2006. Blogging and connecting with educators around the world since 2011, Richard is now a world-recognised educator and blogger on future education trends. He has presented around the world and has been rated in the top fifty world influencers for educational technology use. He currently works in school leadership and is passionate about moving schools forward to better represent the needs of the twenty-first century.

CPSIA information can be obtained
at www.ICGtesting.com
Printed in the USA
FSOW02n2325280217
31393FS